DARK
HORSES
ANNUAL 2022

Marten Julian

Published in 2022 by Marten Julian
69 Highgate, Kendal, Cumbria LA9 4ED
Tel: 01539 741 007
Email: rebecca@martenjulian.com
Copyright © Marten Julian 2022

A catalogue record for this book is available from the British Library.

ISBN: 978-1-7396847-4-7
ISSN: 2633-1713

Cover Design & Layout by Steve Dixon

Cover Photography: Susan Parker

CONTENTS

INTRODUCTION

Hi there!

Thank you for buying this 2022 edition of the *Dark Horses Annual*. I hope that you find it a useful source of reference and enjoyment throughout the course of the season.

As always I have had the support of a talented team to help with the production, without whom this book would not have been possible.

I am greatly indebted to my daughter Rebecca, Steve Dixon, Jodie Standing and Ian Greensill for his painstaking editing work.

You can be kept updated with my latest thoughts on the horses featured in this book either through our *Weekend Card*, which monitors the progress of the Premier List selections every week, or by ringing my line, which is updated every day **(0906 150 1555).**

For details of a subscription or text-based service please speak to Rebecca (01539 74100) or contact her by email **rebecca@martenjulian.com**

I hope that you enjoy a good season.

Bye for now

the Weekend Card

Issued every Wednesday, The *Weekend Card* is our specialist publication offering professional updates, views and recommendations from our select team of experts. Available to download and through the post.

The *Card* covers the next six days racing with the emphasis firmly focused upon the key weekend action. The importance of continuity is the heartbeat of this service, so not only do you receive all the latest news on key horses from our various publications which are declared to run, but also informed comments on selected horses from previous editions.

And we also provide you with honest and accurate feedback on all the previous week's selections – win or lose.

The *Card*, which includes a quick reference sheet, is available as a download, hard copy (by post) or both and you receive a Welcome Pack when you subscribe.

One of the most popular sections in the Card is Marten's Sleeper Section.

This is currently showing a profit to level stakes of 109 points and a return on investment of 57%, while Marten's Look Ahead feature is also showing a profit to level stakes of 68 points thanks to winners that include Sonny Liston 18/1, Atrium 16/1, Reversion 16/1, Gifted Gold 12/1, Lindwall 8/1, Designer 11/2 and long-odds gamble Pride Of Hawridge 9/2 (from 16/1).

THE PREMIER LIST

BAY BRIDGE (4YR BAY COLT)

Trainer:	Sir Michael Stoute
Pedigree:	New Bay – Hayyona (Multiplex)
Form:	34/1111 -
BHA Rating:	112
Optimum Trip:	1m 2f +

Fourth foal half-brother to staying winner Nataleena out of a half-sister to 1m 2f Group 2 winner Shimraan from the family of Prix du Jockey Club runner-up Shamkiyr.

Ran twice as a two-year-old, making his racecourse debut in a 7f novice stakes at Yarmouth in October 2020, slowly away and ridden along from the outset before staying on under determined riding to finish a well-held third.

Reappeared five weeks later in a 1m novice stakes at Kempton, drawn wide in stall 14, again shuffled along from the outset and soon sharing the lead, dropped behind before staying on again in the closing stages to finish an encouraging fourth.

Made his return to action last season in a 1m 2f novice stakes at Newcastle in April, bit keen third of the five runners but moving comfortably, shaken up to take the lead two furlongs from home and quickening clear to beat subsequent dual Meydan winner Al Nefud by five lengths.

Next run came in the competitive 1m 2f London Gold Cup at Newbury, starting a well-supported 11/4 favourite from a mark of 90, raced in mid-division turning for home in seventh before making steady progress through the field to win going away by four lengths from King Frankel.

Raised 15lbs to 105, ran from that mark in October over an extended 1m 2f in a 0-110 Class 2 handicap at York, keen in arrears in the early stages with just two behind him on the home turn, shuffled along and picking up under determined hands and heels driving to assert close home, winning by half a length.

Stepped up to Listed company three weeks later for the 1m 2f Seymour Stakes at Newmarket. Starting a well-backed 6/5 favourite, chased the runaway leader and required strong handling to bridge the gap, asserting close home after looking held for a few strides.

Has been shrewdly kept to a distance short of his pedigree profile, in keeping with the trainer's customary manner of handling his previous top-notchers. Already rated on 112 and will probably find improvement when put over a mile and a half to tackle Group company.

More a dour galloper than a horse with gears, but is just the type with which his trainer excels.

Tough, progressive and with the scope to improve. A likely contender for Group 1 honours.

BAYSIDE BOY (3YR BAY COLT)

Trainer:	Roger Varian
Pedigree:	New Bay – Alava (Anabaa)
Form:	12133 -
BHA Rating:	114
Optimum Trip:	1m +

Cost 200,000gns as a yearling and an eighth foal half-brother to Group 2 Huxley Stakes winner Forest Ranger, four-race winner Home Cummins and 1m maiden winner Gaudi.

Very likeable son of Prix du Jockey Club winner New Bay, who made an immediate impression when overcoming a tardy start to land a 7f novice stakes at Newbury in July, travelling in mid-division and looking held approaching the final furlong before producing a turn of foot, taking him three and a quarter lengths clear of 1/3 favourite Find.

Raised in class just over a month later, back at Newbury for a 7f Listed contest, better away this time, cajoled along at halfway and looked the likely winner but pipped on the nod by Masekela, who had previously run Native Trail to a short head.

Appeared just less than a month later in the Group 2 Champagne Stakes at Doncaster, keen fourth of four early on, then more settled at halfway and thereafter responded to firm driving to beat Reach For The Moon in the last few strides, winning by a head.

Up again in grade next time for the Group 1 Dewhurst Stakes, held up behind travelling well, made headway and stayed on tenaciously into third, closing at the line.

Final start came in the Group 1 Futurity Trophy at Doncaster, again held up going well at halfway but short of room, stuck on gamely to finish third, one and three-quarter lengths behind the winner.

Very progressive and consistent, but needs to learn to relax in the preliminaries and early stages of his races. Trainer says he will probably be a miler, but he is bred to stay further if he learns to settle.

May struggle to beat the best, but included here in the firm belief that he will try his utmost at all times and appeals as the sort to reward each-way support when competing at the highest level.

Will not be disgraced in the 2000 Guineas.

CHING SHIH (3YR BAY FILLY)

Trainer:	David Simcock
Pedigree:	Lope De Vega – Madame Chiang (Archipenko)
Form:	31 -
BHA Rating:	N/A
Optimum Trip:	1m 4f +

Third foal and a half-sister to 1m 4f Listed winner Oriental Mystique and a 7f AW winner. Dam, who loved heavy ground, won the Group 1 Fillies & Mares Stakes at Ascot from a strong family of stayers.

Caught the eye on her debut in a slowly run 1m maiden at Newcastle in October, taken back at start and racing a little keen, nudged along at halfway and kept on to finish third, beaten three and a quarter lengths.

Out again just 15 days later, contesting a 1m novice stakes on soft ground at Newbury, again keen early stages just off the lead, switched for a clear run at halfway and soon quickened to go clear and win by four lengths from promising newcomer Geri Hatrick, with now 79-rated Cave Diver a further head away in third.

Comes from an excellent mud-loving family and looks the type who can earn black type in the autumn. Classy, has a turn of foot and will stay a mile and a half, perhaps beyond.

CUMULONIMBUS (3YR CHESTNUT COLT)

Trainer:	Charlie Fellowes
Pedigree:	Night Of Thunder – Queen's Novel (King's Best)
Form:	3 -
BHA Rating:	N/A
Optimum Trip:	1m 4f +

Second foal of a 1m 3f AW winning half-sister to four-race winner Mansfield and three AW winners from 1m to 1m 4f.

Sole start came in a 7f maiden stakes at Doncaster in October, steadied start and keen, travelled better at halfway but short of room in the middle of the pack, switched to nearside of the group and shuffled along on the rails and stayed on very well to finish a closing third to Jimi Hendrix and now 82-rated Beluga Gold.

Shaped like the best horse in the race and sure to win races, possibly progressing to quite a high level. Will stay ten furlongs, and probably further.

DARK VEGA (3YR BAY FILLY)

Trainer:	Jessica Harrington
Pedigree:	Lope De Vega – Dream Club (Dansili)
Form:	1 -
BHA Rating:	87
Optimum Trip:	1m 4f +

Lope De Vega sixth foal and a half-sister to 2m Flat and hurdle winner Upgraded, and Flat and hurdle winners Dream Point, Prince Charmin' and Darkened. Dam unraced daughter of Dansili and a half-sister to 2m 4f Group 1 Prix du Cadran winner Invermark.

Could hardly be more stoutly bred, so did well to win a 7f maiden at the Curragh by a neck from Boundless Ocean, steadily away from the gate but travelling comfortably in arrears, nudged along three furlongs from home and made relentless progress, getting up close home to win by a neck.

Rated 87 and clearly has something to find to be competitive at the highest level, but has a pedigree laden with stamina and may well bridge the gap once she is asked to tackle a distance of ground.

Has the potential to become a very useful staying filly.

DUKE DE SESSA (3YR BAY COLT)

Trainer:	Dermot Weld
Pedigree:	Lope De Vega – Dark Crusader (Cape Cross)
Form:	3161 - 3
BHA Rating:	106
Optimum Trip:	1m +

Third foal half-brother to a 1m 2f AW winner out of a Group-placed 1m 6f Melrose Stakes winning half-sister to 1m 5f Listed winner Naughty Or Nice and useful middle-distance performer Cailini Alainn.

Made his debut in a 7f maiden stakes at Galway in July, slowly into his stride and travelling well at halfway, went wide around the home turn before coming with a late surge to finish a fast-closing third, beaten just half a length by the winner.

Reappeared just less than a month later in a 1m maiden at the Curragh, better away and tucked in just off the pace, travelling well in fifth at halfway, before taking the lead two furlongs out and drawing clear to beat Adonis by four and three-quarter lengths.

Stepped up in class the following month for the Group 1 National Stakes, dropped back to 7f, but never competitive and not given a hard time once held, beaten ten and a half lengths by Native Trail.

Returned to form stepped up to 1m 1f for the Group 3 Eyrefield Stakes at Leopardstown, drawn wide in stall 11 and soon behind, still last home turn and very wide before passing the entire field to win going away by half a length.

Not disgraced when third to Piz Badile on his return in the 1m 2f Group 3 Ballysax Stakes at Leopardstown in April, doing his best work late in the day.

Form may not be top class, but only a talented colt could have won in this manner. Has a formidable turn of foot and will be suited to a strongly run race over a mile but will stay a mile and a quarter.

Trainer has spoken in terms of the Irish 2,000 Guineas but may be one to consider for the Derby or Irish Derby.

Looks very tough.

DUN NA SEAD (3YR CHESTNUT FILLY)

Trainer:	Kieran Cotter
Pedigree:	Starspangledbanner – Alice Thornton (Hurricane Run)
Form:	1 -
BHA Rating:	N/A
Optimum Trip:	5f +

Second foal half-sister to winner Lord Dudley out of AW winning half-sister to winners from 5f to 1m 1f from the family of Oaks winner Lady Carla.

Made all to win a 5f maiden at the Curragh in late September with ease, from subsequent winners in second and third.

Not seen out again, but spoken of in glowing terms afterwards by her handler and could prove competitive at a decent level.

Very speedy.

LIONEL (3YR CHESTNUT COLT)

Trainer:	David Menuisier
Pedigree:	Lope De Vega – Gretchen (Galileo)
Form:	2 -
BHA Rating:	N/A
Optimum Trip:	1m 4f +

Second foal of Group 2 Park Hill Stakes winner Gretchen from the family of Irish St Leger winner Duncan and 2m 2f Group 2 Doncaster Cup winner Samuel.

Sole start came on heavy ground in a 1m novice stakes at Newbury in October, soon settled in arrears but quite keen and green, tucked away on rails before being sharply switched right for a clear run and found a surge to swoop past his rivals and hit the front, until caught close home by Zain Nights.

Fourth, beaten four lengths, now rated on 74 suggesting the winner ran to a mark in the low 80s.

Looks an exciting prospect for middle-distance/staying races and evidently acts well in soft ground. Appears to have a turn of foot.

MAGISTERIAL (3YR BAY COLT)

Trainer:	John Gosden
Pedigree:	Frankel – Hoity Toity (Darshaan)
Form:	41 -
BHA Rating:	N/A
Optimum Trip:	1m 4f +

Twelfth foal and full brother to extended 1m 3f novice stakes winner Flaunt and a three-parts brother to Group 1 Matron Stakes and Coronation Stakes winner Lillie Langtry, and half-brother to Listed winner Count Of Limonade, Danilovna and Howman.

Made his debut in a 1m maiden stakes at Newmarket in September, steadily away and soon in arrears, made steady progress at halfway and plugged on steadily to finish a closing fourth, beaten two lengths by the useful Subastar.

Reappeared the following month in a 1m novice stakes at Haydock, soon racing just off the pace, turned for home in fifth taken wide in the straight, shuffled along two furlongs out and took a while to pick up before beating subsequent winner Splendent by a length and a half, with now-rated 76 Just Wonder a further three and a quarter lengths back in third.

Evidently learnt a lot from his debut and has a professional way of going about his business.

Bred for middle distances and looks another potential high-class staying prospect for his owner.

NOBEL (3YR CHESTNUT COLT)

Trainer:	Andrew Balding
Pedigree:	Lope De Vega – Starlet (Sea The Stars)
Form:	1 -
BHA Rating:	N/A
Optimum Trip:	1m 2f +

Fourth foal and 835,000gns yearling half-brother to Listed winner Raakib Alhawa and 7f Group 3 winner Love Locket out of lightly raced 1m 4f winner Starlet from the family of 10-race dual Derby winner High Chaparral.

Lived up to trainer's high expectations when winning a 1m novice stakes at Kempton in December, well away and soon tracking leader on the rails, shaken up to take the lead early in the straight and stretched out to beat Western Writer by three lengths with plenty in hand.

Fourth, beaten six and a half lengths, now rated on 62 which suggests the winner ran to a mark in the mid to high 70s, but the trainer spoke of the horse in glowing terms after the race.

Unfortunately sustained a setback early in the year but expected to take high rank if all is well upon his return. Should stay a mile and a half.

TRAILA (4YR CHESTNUT GELDING)

Trainer:	Sir Michael Stoute
Pedigree:	Australia – Waila (Notnowcato)
Form:	51 -
BHA Rating:	N/A
Optimum Trip:	1m 2f +

Second foal of 1m 4f Listed winner Waila, from the family of Group 1 winners Crystal Ocean and Hillstar from the family of a Poule d'Essai des Pouliches winner.

Unraced at two, made his belated racecourse debut in a 1m 2f novice stakes at Leicester in April, equipped with a noseband – unusually for this yard – travelled comfortably and kept galloping all the way to the line under a considerate ride, beaten three lengths.

Not seen out again until October, made favourite for an extended 1m 1f novice stakes at Wolverhampton. Again wearing a noseband, pushed up to the front rank and took the lead in the straight and battled on well to hold subsequent triple-winner Famous Star.

Should stay middle distances and has the potential to improve way beyond this level. Appears to have a good attitude.

the Weekend Card

Issued every Wednesday, The *Weekend Card* is our specialist publication offering professional updates, views and recommendations from our select team of experts. Available to download and through the post.

The *Card* covers the next six days racing with the emphasis firmly focused upon the key weekend action. The importance of continuity is the heartbeat of this service, so not only do you receive all the latest news on key horses from our various publications which are declared to run, but also informed comments on selected horses from previous editions.

And we also provide you with honest and accurate feedback on all the previous week's selections – win or lose.

The *Card*, which includes a quick reference sheet, is available as a download, hard copy (by post) or both and you receive a Welcome Pack when you subscribe.

One of the most popular sections in the Card is Marten's Sleeper Section.

This is currently showing a profit to level stakes of 109 points and a return on investment of 57%, while Marten's Look Ahead feature is also showing a profit to level stakes of 68 points thanks to winners that include Sonny Liston 18/1, Atrium 16/1, Reversion 16/1, Gifted Gold 12/1, Lindwall 8/1, Designer 11/2 and long-odds gamble Pride Of Hawridge 9/2 (from 16/1).

Order online at www.martenjulian.com or call the office on 01539 741 007

THE DARK HANDICAPPERS

AASSER (3YR BLACK COLT)

Trainer:	Karl Burke
Pedigree:	Dabirsim – Iffraja (Iffraaj)
Form:	221-
BHA Rating:	80
Optimum Trip:	6f +

Progressive son of Prix Morny winner Dabirsim out of a daughter of Iffraaj from the family of Group 1 winner Pipalong. Made his debut in 7f maiden stakes at Wolverhampton in November, chasing winner in the final half-mile and keeping on well to be beaten a length by Anatomic.

Reappeared later that month in a 7f maiden back at Wolverhampton and led from an early stage, looking the winner entering the final furlong until caught in the closing strides by Checkandchallenge.

Dropped back to 6f for a novice stakes, again at Wolverhampton just over a month later, and missed the break but soon recovered the ground, raced handy and quickened to lead inside the final furlong to win by a length.

Showed an impressive turn of foot in victory and is evidently extremely effective at 6f, but has the pedigree to stay further. May progress beyond handicaps.

AL HUSN (3YR BAY FILLY)

Trainer:	Roger Varian
Pedigree:	Dubawi – Hadaatha (Sea The Stars)
Form:	041 -
BHA Rating:	82
Optimum Trip:	1m 4f +

Fourth foal and half-sister to a 1m 3f winner out of a half-sister to 2m winner Itlaaq from the family of the useful Ivan Luis.

Showed progressive form in her three starts, racing keenly until dropping away on her debut in a 7f maiden stakes at Newmarket in September.

Displayed significant improvement just under a month later in a 7f novice stakes at Kempton, very slowly away but soon travelling well in arrears before being switched wide in the straight and quickening through the field to finish never nearer in fourth. Finished full of running and would have won over another furlong.

Final run came in a 1m novice stakes at Kempton in November, better away on this occasion and shuffled along throughout until switched to challenge a furlong from home, instantly quickening to lead and win by one and three-quarter lengths, clearly relishing the step up to a mile.

Could prove extremely well treated on 82, especially when stepped up in trip. An exciting prospect.

CANTERBURY BELL (3YR BAY FILLY)

Trainer:	William Haggas
Pedigree:	Ribchester – Lavender Lane (Shamardal)
Form:	001 -
BHA Rating:	70
Optimum Trip:	1m

Second foal and half-sister to 1m 2f Listed winner Lilac Road out of a winning half-sister to black type winners over 1m 2f and 1m 4f.

Made her racecourse debut and quietly backed for a 1m novices' stakes at Ascot in September but ran very green throughout and finished well behind, beaten 13 and three-quarter lengths by the winner.

Still looked green later that month in an extended 1m maiden fillies' race at Nottingham, shuffled along in mid-division and staying on at one pace to finish ninth of 13. Reported afterwards to have lost her right-hind shoe.

Stepped up markedly on those efforts when dropped in trip for 7f novice stakes at Newmarket in October. Raced apart from the main group on the near side, handling the soft ground well, and up with the pace in second. Nudged along 3f out, looked held 2f out but kept on well to finish a short-head second to Silver Kitten but was awarded the race afterwards.

Appropriately assessed on a mark of 70 on a line through Silver Kitten, rated 73, but leaves the impression that she will prove significantly superior to her mark. A slow learner but clearly suited by soft ground.

DANE FETE (3YR BAY GELDING)

Trainer:	Gavin Cromwell
Pedigree:	Kodiac – Village Fete (Singspiel)
Form:	000 -
BHA Rating:	N/A
Optimum Trip:	1m +

Half-brother to six winners over distances up to 1m 6f out of a middle-distance-winning half-sister to Grade 3 winner Trade Fair.

Made his debut in an extended 5f median auction maiden at Navan in October, very slowly away and soon struggling in last place, still green 2f out but responded to strong urgings to make up ground in the final furlong.

Reappeared in a 1m maiden stakes at Dundalk just over a fortnight later. Again slowly into stride, still well behind turning for home, wobbled around in the straight before picking up in the final furlong, beaten just three and a half lengths at the line.

Returned over the same course and distance a fortnight later and always behind, but not given a hard time in the closing stages to finish with two of his 13 rivals behind him.

Performances have concealed rather more than they have revealed, and could be of great interest in a low-grade handicap once he acquires a mark.

DENNING (3YR CHESTNUT GELDING)

Trainer:	Sir Mark Prescott
Pedigree:	Recorder – Undress (Dalakhani)
Form:	0000 -
BHA Rating:	66
Optimum Trip:	1m 4f +

Half-brother to a 6f winner out of a daughter of Dalakhani from the family of Oaks winner Casual Look.

Made his debut in a 6f maiden stakes at Doncaster in November. Lobbed along in last and outpaced despite urgings from halfway, finishing nine and a half lengths behind the winner.

Reappeared 18 days later in a 7f maiden at Kempton. Drawn on the wide outside in stall 14, soon switched to the back of the pack, noticeably keen turning for home. Out of his ground on the final turn but started to pick up nicely before being hampered approaching the final furlong, catching the eye with a late flourish.

Came out again at the same track five days later, in a 1m novice stakes, well away on this occasion and travelling in the front rank. Fifth turning for home, shuffled along 2f out and lost his place in the final furlong under considerate handling.

Ran again in a 1m novice stakes at Lingfield in December. Drawn wide in stall 10 and soon lost his place but raced keenly in rear and still behind 4f out before travelling better on the turn for home and shaped in most encouraging fashion in the straight, finishing strongly.

Has displayed more than sufficient ability to win a race from his opening mark, notably when stepped up in trip.

DESIGNER (3YR CHESTNUT FILLY)

Trainer:	John Butler
Pedigree:	Pearl Secret – Curly Come Home (Notnowcato)
Form:	4201 -
BHA Rating:	82
Optimum Trip:	5f +

Cheaply bought half-sister to 7f winner Lofty out of a middle-distance-winning relative to Group 3 winner Ziria.

Made her debut in a 7f novice stakes at Kempton in August, slowly away and soon behind, made some progress on the turn for home and looked promising when coming with a run in the straight staying on to finish fourth.

Reappeared the following month in a 6f novice stakes at Newcastle, better away on this occasion and soon settled just off the pace on the far side of the group. Made pleasing progress approaching the final two furlongs and stayed on well to the line, finishing second and nicely clear of the third.

Raised significantly in class 15 days later for the 6f Group 3 Firth Of Clyde Fillies' Stakes at Ayr, starting 66/1 but outrunning those odds, in the front rank at halfway and looking a threat until fading quickly inside the final furlong, beaten six lengths at the line.

Dropped back to 5f for a Class 4 novice stakes at Chester in October, drawn unfavourably in stall seven, soon bustled along and chasing the leader, still second turning for home but took the lead inside the final furlong and kept on well to win narrowly by a head, proving well suited to the soft ground.

Dropped from 83 to 82 following this success, looks ideally poised to win a valuable sprint handicap at some point this season. Appears to have a turn of foot.

DISSOCIATE (3YR BAY FILLY)

Trainer:	Paddy Twomey
Pedigree:	Almanzor – Party Animal (Makfi)
Form:	201 -
BHA Rating:	N/A
Optimum Trip:	1m +

First foal of a middle-distance-placed half-sister to useful performers Observational and Party Line from a decent French family.

Made her debut in a 6f maiden contest at the Curragh in May. Towards rear nudged along and a bit short of room at halfway, weaved her way through in the final quarter-mile to come with a strong challenge inside the final furlong, beaten half a length at the line.

Reappeared a few days later in a 7f maiden fillies race at Leopardstown, soon pushed into the lead, led home turn but lost place in the straight to finish tenth of 14. Was found to be slightly lame afterwards.

Not seen out again until late October, nicely backed for a 7f fillies maiden at the Curragh. Drawn widest of all in stall 27, raced on the nearside and soon made progress to join the front rank. Took the lead 2f out and drew clear to win by three and a half lengths.

Has not yet been given a mark but has the potential to prove better than a handicapper. Handles soft ground and should stay at least a mile.

EAGLE'S WAY (3YR CHESTNUT GELDING)

Trainer:	Sir Mark Prescott
Pedigree:	Gleneagles – Martlet (Dansili)
Form:	000 -
BHA Rating:	67
Optimum Trip:	1m 2f +

Cost 95,000gns as a yearling and a three-parts brother to lightly raced 1m 4f maiden winner Franklet and a half-brother to 7f handicap winner Wolflet out of a 1m 2f / 1m 4f Galtres Stakes winning daughter of Dansili.

Has shaped with distinct promise in three runs, starting in a 7f maiden at Doncaster, went right at the start, keen and then staying on under hands and heels. Again showed ability next time in a 7f maiden at Kempton in November, drawn wide in stall 12 and on the outside of the field turning for home before plugging on at the finish.

Revealed a little more on his final start at Wolverhampton later that month, fifth early stages and nudged out to finish seventh of nine, beaten seven and three-quarter lengths.

Has been brought along quietly but looks capable of winning races off 67, with likely improvement when stepped up to 1m 2f, possibly further.

EDUCATOR (3YR BROWN COLT)

Trainer:	William Haggas
Pedigree:	Deep Impact – Diploma (Dubawi)
Form:	021 -
BHA Rating:	85
Optimum Trip:	1m 2f +

Full brother to 1m 2f winner Portfolio out of a Listed-winning half-sister to the useful Elector from a useful family.

Made his debut in a 7f maiden stakes at Newbury in August. Well away, ran green and soon struggling to keep his place, soon dropped back and finished well in arrears, beaten just over 14 lengths at the line.

Shaped much better the following month in a 1m maiden stakes at Goodwood. Very well away and soon sharing the lead, turned for home in second and took a narrow lead approaching the final furlong but caught final strides despite staying on well.

Reappeared 18 days later in a 1m novice stakes at Haydock, equipped with sheepskins for the first time, well away and settled in second, racing willingly, looked held until steadily overcoming the leader inside the final furlong and kept on gamely to win by a neck.

Acts well on quick ground and appears to be crying out for a step up in trip. Could progress beyond handicaps.

ELECTRESS (3YR BAY FILLY)

Trainer:	Ralph Beckett
Pedigree:	Galileo – Just The Judge (Lawman)
Form:	032 -
BHA Rating:	80
Optimum Trip:	1m 4f +

Third foal and half-sister to winners over 1m 2f and 1m 4f, out of Irish 1,000 Guineas and EP Taylor Stakes winner Just The Judge, a daughter of Lawman.

Made her debut in a 7f maiden stakes at Newbury in August, slowly away but travelling well off the pace at halfway, soon pushed along nearside of the group, no further progress but shaped well.

Next run came four weeks later in a 1m maiden stakes at Goodwood, settled just off the pace in third five lengths off the leaders turning for home, stayed on strongly to challenge but joined near the line to finish a half-length third.

Reappeared just over a month later in a 1m 1f novice stakes back at Goodwood in October, soon raced prominently in third and chased along in the straight, took a while to get going before picking up strongly inside the final furlong, just failing to win by a short head.

Bred to relish middle distances and is sure to prove superior to her current mark.

GORDONS AURA (3YR BAY GELDING)

Trainer:	Sir Mark Prescott
Pedigree:	Golden Horn – Sequined (Street Cry)
Form:	500 -
BHA Rating:	66
Optimum Trip:	1m 2f +

Third foal half-brother to US turf and AW winner Succeedandsurpass out of a winning daughter of Fillies' Mile winner and Irish Oaks runner-up Sunspangled.

Encouraging first season, starting in a 7f novice stakes at Kempton in October, slowly away and soon chased along, stayed in touch throughout and still strong at the line. Returned there a fortnight later, again for a 7f novice, better away and keen, seventh turning for home, shuffled along two furlongs out and again keeping on well to finish ninth of 14.

Had more use made of him in a 1m maiden at Lingfield in late November, well away and soon handy on the outside of the field, second at halfway but forced wide on home turn before staying on strongly to the line, beaten five lengths by a useful winner.

Probably reasonably treated on an opening mark of 66 and has already shown enough to suggest races will come his way. Looks a genuine sort.

HOLIDAY (3YR BAY COLT)

Trainer:	Richard Hannon
Pedigree:	Time Test – Precious Angel (Excelebration)
Form:	640 -
BHA Rating:	72
Optimum Trip:	1m +

First foal of a half-sister to 6f Group 2 winner Infamous Angel from the family of Listed winner Sgt Pepper.

Shaped with promise in his three runs last season, improving on his debut effort when fourth in a 7f novice stakes at Sandown in September, slowly away before making progress in the straight, stumbling badly a furlong out and then staying on again in the final furlong.

Stepped up in class next time for a valuable 6f sales race at Newmarket in October, again slowly away and finishing in mid-division 19th of 28.

Bred to improve over a mile and starts his campaign from a reasonable mark.

HONKY TONK MAN (3YR BAY COLT)

Trainer:	Roger Charlton
Pedigree:	Tamayuz – Dance Hall Girl (Dansili)
Form:	611 -
BHA Rating:	88
Optimum Trip:	1m +

Seventh foal from a good family, a half-brother to five winners including Listed winner Tashweeq and HMS President.

Ran very green on his debut in a 6f contest at Newbury in May, losing many lengths at the start and allowed to come home in his own time, last of six.

Did not appear again until late October in a 7f novice stakes at Lingfield, drawn wide in stall 12 but soon travelling keenly just behind the leaders, turned for home in fourth and went wide round the bend before coming with a well-timed challenge to win going away by two lengths.

Reappeared a fortnight later in a 7f novice stakes at Newcastle, again keen and up with the leaders, second at halfway, found a turn of foot approaching the final furlong to win comfortably by one and a quarter lengths.

Bred to suit a mile, possibly further, and expected to improve beyond handicaps. Looks potentially useful.

MACCHIAVELLO (3YR BAY GELDING)

Trainer:	Karl Burke
Pedigree:	No Nay Never – Mona Vale (Zoffany)
Form:	453 -
BHA Rating:	72
Optimum Trip:	6f +

Not cheap at £300,000 as a two-year-old, the first foal of an unraced half-sister to a middle-distance-winning daughter of Zoffany from the family of Group and Graded winners.

Started odds-on for his debut in a 6f novice stakes at Redcar in October, showing early pace before fading into fourth inside the final furlong.

Next run came in a 7f maiden stakes at Wolverhampton in November, drawn wide in stall 10 and refused to settle, pulling very hard in the first half-mile, turning for home in mid-division and soon pushed along but found little in the closing stages to finish fifth.

Again raced far too freely on his third start in a 6f novice stakes at Newcastle in December, racing up with the pace and leading at halfway but kept on better this time to finish a well held third.

Has subsequently been gelded and evidently rated better than his form reflects. Will need to learn to settle if he is to realise his full potential.

OLIVETTI (3YR BAY GELDING)

Trainer:	Marcus Tregoning
Pedigree:	Showcasing – Tschierschen (Acclamation)
Form:	665 -
BHA Rating:	70
Optimum Trip:	6f ?

Second foal half-brother to 1m winner Perotto out of a 5f-winning half-sister to Group-placed Gallagher from the family of 7f winner Roodeye.

Made his debut in a 6f novice stakes at Newbury in July, ducked right at the start and soon racing freely, shuffled along vigorously at halfway and responded well to finish never-nearer sixth.

Came out again just 10 days later in a 6f maiden stakes at Goodwood, again lugging right at the start and racing keenly, tucked in on the rails and progress at halfway but did not get a clear run and switched right inside final furlong, staying on late to finish sixth.

Dropped to 5f for his final start in a maiden at Sandown in August, quickly away on this occasion and showed good speed until headed a furlong out and dropped away under considerate handling to finish last of five.

Bred to stay further but needs to settle better if he is to do so. Probably superior to his mark and will be placed to advantage by his gifted handler.

OMNISCIENT (3YR BAY GELDING)

Trainer:	Sir Mark Prescott
Pedigree:	Mukhadram – Miss Dashwood (Dylan Thomas)
Form:	05 -
BHA Rating:	N/A
Optimum Trip:	1m 2f +

Not yet handicapped but bred to thrive over a distance of ground, a three-parts brother to 1m 4f winner Loving Dash and a half-brother to Queen's Vase winner Dashing Willoughby. Dam a winner up to 1m 4f and a half-sister to 1m 2f Group 1 Prix de l'Opera winner Speedy Boarding.

Didn't give much away in two starts, when very slowly away and always behind but keeping on steadily in a 7f novice stakes at Kempton in September, and then fifth of six in a 7f novice stakes at Chelmsford. Looked very green on his debut, wobbling around the bend, but showed more maturity next time, racing competitively in arrears upsides with a rival in the closing stages.

Has run to a mark in the low 60s and his next race should secure that figure. Probably prove suited to 1m 2f, or further.

POETIKEL PIECE (3YR BAY FILLY)

Trainer:	Adrian Nicholls
Pedigree:	Mayson – Nardin (Royal Applause)
Form:	600 -
BHA Rating:	60
Optimum Trip:	5f +

Half-sister to Italian sprint winner from the family of 1m Listed winner Party Boss and Triumph Hurdle winner Countrywide Flame.

Made her debut in a 6f maiden stakes at Haydock in September, ducked right at the start but soon up with the pace, travelling well halfway before fading inside the final furlong under tender handling.

Raised in class for a 6f Listed race the following month, showed early speed nearside of the group, still travelling comfortably at halfway, pushed along 2f out and lost place soon afterwards, shaping better than her finishing position would suggest.

Dropped to 5f for her final start in a novice stakes at Catterick, raced with one other on the inside of the track and again displayed early speed before being left behind inside the final furlong.

Not short of pace and looks a handy sort for northern sprint handicaps.

SPIRIT OF UAE (3YR BAY GELDING)

Trainer:	Ed Walker
Pedigree:	Postponed – Classic Code (Galileo)
Form:	00 - 4
BHA Rating:	70
Optimum Trip:	1m 4f +

Second foal of an unraced full sister to Group-placed winner Tamarind Cove from the family of Irish 1,000 Guineas winner Saoire.

Began his career in an extended 1m maiden stakes at Nottingham in October, always behind but started to make headway in the straight until squeezed for room and blocked in his run 2f out.

Next appeared in an extended 1m 1f novice stakes at Wolverhampton in December, again racing in arrears and finishing with just three of his 12 rivals behind him.

Stepped up to 1m 4f for a novice stakes at Kempton in January, better away on this occasion and raced just off the pace in third, travelling quite well four furlongs out, every chance in the straight and looking a threat 2f out before fading away inside the final furlong.

Had a progressive profile in these three runs and nicely poised to win from his opening mark over a distance of ground. Has been gelded since his last run.

VINTAGE CHOICE (3YR CHESTNUT GELDING)

Trainer:	William Haggas
Pedigree:	Lope De Vega – Effervesce (Galileo)
Form:	31 -
BHA Rating:	N/A
Optimum Trip:	1m 2f +

Cost 310,000gns as a yearling and the sixth foal half-brother to useful winner Persuasion and Listed winner Cristal Fizz out of a winning half-sister to Group 3 winner Hitchens.

Made his debut in the prestigious Convivial Maiden Stakes at York in August, soon behind and shuffled along at halfway, short of room 2f out, switched for a clear run but again intimidated inside the final furlong before keeping on bravely to finish third.

Reappeared just over a month later in a 7f maiden stakes at Redcar, well supported in the market and soon up with the pace, looking in trouble 2f out before staying on strongly to get up and win in the final stride.

Found 7f an inadequate test last season and is bred to come into his own over 1m 2f or more. Likely to receive a mark in the mid-80s.

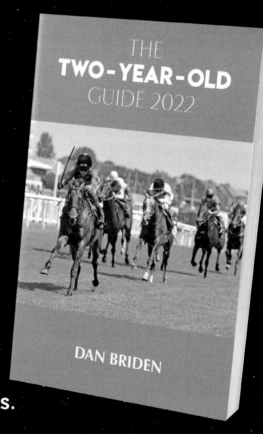

THE DARK HORSES

AL SAHARA (3YR BAY FILLY)

Trainer:	Charlie Appleby
Pedigree:	Galileo – Lumiere (Shamardal)
Form:	Unraced
Optimum Trip:	1m +

Second foal of very useful Cheveley Park Stakes winner Lumiere and a half-sister to Listed winner Highland Avenue. Dam is a full sister to Canadian 1m 2f Grade 1 winner Sheikha Reika.

Highly regarded by her trainer and bred to excel over a mile or more.

ANTILIA (3YR BAY FILLY)

Trainer:	Joseph O'Brien
Pedigree:	Fastnet Rock – Could It Be (Galileo)
Form:	Unraced
Optimum Trip:	1m 2f +

Fifth foal and a three-parts sister to useful 1m winner Mubariz. Dam an unraced sister to Group 1 winners Misty For Me and Ballydoyle.

Bred for middle distances.

CAROMIL (3YR BAY FILLY)

Trainer:	Jessica Harrington
Pedigree:	Sea The Stars – Greenisland (Fasliyev)
Form:	Unraced
Optimum Trip:	1m +

Seventh foal and a full sister to UAE Listed winner Boerhan and a half-sister to three winners including 6f Listed winner Shamshon. Dam winning half-sister to 6f Group 1 Cheveley Park Stakes winner Millisle.

Bred to be effective at a mile but should stay further.

CHAMPAGNE (3YR BAY FILLY)

Trainer:	Aidan O'Brien
Pedigree:	Galileo – Red Evie (Intikhab)
Form:	Unraced
Optimum Trip:	1m +

Ninth foal from an excellent family, a full sister to seven winners including three times Group and Grade 1 winner Found and Group 3 winners Magical Dream, Divinely and Best In The World (the dam of Snowfall).

The dam Red Evie won nine of her 15 starts including the Group 1 Matron Stakes and the Lockinge Stakes.

Superbly bred and should appreciate trips of a mile or more.

DAIQUIRI DREAM (3YR BAY FILLY)

Trainer:	Ralph Beckett
Pedigree:	Dubawi – Cocktail Queen (Motivator)
Form:	Unraced
Optimum Trip:	1m 4f +

Second foal and a full sister to 1m winner Tom Collins out of a useful UK and French middle-distance Group 2/3 winner from the family of useful performer Gold Prince and the dam of an Italian 2,000 Guineas winner.

Described by her trainer as a big tall filly who has needed time. Bred to thrive over middle distances.

DEFERRED (3YR CHESTNUT COLT)

Trainer:	Roger Varian
Pedigree:	Postponed – Platinum Pearl (Shamardal)
Form:	Unraced
Optimum Trip:	1m +

Third living foal and three-parts brother to Listed winner Invitational out of a winning half-sister to useful performers Samminder and Queen's Pearl from the speedy family of Prix Morny winner First Waltz.

Should stay a mile but has plenty of pace in his pedigree.

DENVER (3YR CHESTNUT COLT)

Trainer:	Aidan O'Brien
Pedigree:	Galileo – Halfway To Heaven (Pivotal)
Form:	Unraced
Optimum Trip:	1m +

Seventh foal and a full brother to 12-race winner Magical, five-race winner Rhododendron and 1m 2f Group 3 winner Flying The Flag. Dam won three times at Group 1 level and is a daughter of King's Stand winner Cassandra Go.

One of the best bred horses in this section and reported to be showing he has inherited some of the family's ability.

ELITE ETOILE (3YR BAY COLT)

Trainer:	Jonathan Portman
Pedigree:	Vadamos – Way To The Stars (Dansili)
Form:	Unraced
Optimum Trip:	1m 4f +

Half-brother to useful winner Precision Storm out of a half-sister to five-time South African Grade 1 winner Dancer's Daughter, Group 3 winner Diktatorial and 1m 1f winner Stands To Reason from the family of South African 6f Grade 2 winner Search Party.

Looks well bought at £16,000 as a yearling and bred to stay middle distances although not devoid of speed in his family.

Said by his trainer to have needed time.

EXPRESS WAY (3YR BAY FILLY)

Trainer:	Paddy Twomey
Pedigree:	Dark Angel – Alluring Park (Green Desert)
Form:	Unraced
Optimum Trip:	1m + ?

Eleventh foal and a half-sister to no fewer than eight winners including 2012 Oaks winner Was, Group 3 winner Douglas Macarthur, 1m 6f Group 2 winner Amhran Na Bhfiann, 7f winner Al Naamah and Listed winner Janood.

Has a top-class middle-distance pedigree and expected to do well for her low-profile trainer.

EYAZIYA (3YR BAY FILLY)

Trainer:	Dermot Weld
Pedigree:	Sea The Stars – Eshera (Oratorio)
Form:	Unraced
Optimum Trip:	1m 4f +

Daughter of Sea The Stars and a half-sister to two winners out of a Listed winning half-sister to Group 2 winner Eziyra from a top-class family.

Bred to thrive over middle distances.

FENNELA (3YR BAY FILLY)

Trainer:	Jessica Harrington
Pedigree:	Sea The Stars – Green Room (Theatrical)
Form:	Unraced
Optimum Trip:	1m 4f +

Twelfth foal and very stoutly bred full sister to 1m 2f winner Signe and a half-sister to six winners including Group 1 Prix Jean Prat winner Lord Shanakill, 1m 4f winner Forever Together and 1m winner Together Forever.

Dam unraced half-sister to US Group 1 winner Spanish Fern.

Will relish a distance of ground.

FIORELLINA (3YR BAY FILLY)

Trainer:	Dermot Weld
Pedigree:	Galileo – Sapphire (Medicean)
Form:	Unraced
Optimum Trip:	1m 4f

Fifth foal and a full sister to 1m 2f winner Federica Sophia and a half-sister to winners Kiss For A Jewel and Jewel Maker.

Dam won six of her 11 starts including two at Group 3 level and Group 2 Champion Fillies' and Mares' Stakes from the family of Group 1 winner Free Eagle and Search For A Song.

Bred in the purple and should thrive over middle distances.

FIRST EMPEROR (3YR BAY COLT)

Trainer:	Donnacha O'Brien
Pedigree:	Galileo – Sky Lantern (Red Clubs)
Form:	Unraced
Optimum Trip:	1m 2f ?

First foal of four-time Group 1 winner Sky Lantern and a three-parts brother to Group 1 Falmouth Stakes winner Snow Lantern and a half-brother to winners over a mile and 1m 6f.

Could hardly be better bred and should prove effective at 1m 2f, possibly further.

GLAMOURISTA (3YR CHESTNUT FILLY)

Trainer:	Jim Bolger
Pedigree:	Dawn Approach – My Fere Lady (Mr Greeley)
Form:	Unraced
Optimum Trip:	1m

Fourth foal and a full sister to 1m winner Feminista out of a daughter of Mr Greeley from the family of useful US Grade 3 winners Got The Last Laugh and Theresa's Tizzy.

Should prove effective over a mile.

GULLIVER'S TRAVELS (3YR BAY COLT)

Trainer:	Aidan O'Brien
Pedigree:	Galileo – Prudenzia (Dansili)
Form:	Unraced
Optimum Trip:	1m 4f +

Cost €2,000,000 as a yearling and the ninth foal full brother to three winners, including Group 1 Australian winner Magic Wand, and closely related to Irish Oaks winner Chicquita and a half-sister to three other winners including Group 3 level. Dam won twice from five starts including 1m 3f big Listed race in France.

Bred to thrive over middle distances.

HEATHEN (3YR BAY COLT)

Trainer:	Ed Dunlop
Pedigree:	Lope De Vega – Great Heavens (Galileo)
Form:	Unraced
Optimum Trip:	1m 4f +

Sixth foal and half-brother to five winners over a mile and more including 2m winner Dubhe, 1m 4f Group 3 winner Thunder Drum and 1m winner Sun Bear. Dam, winner of the Irish Oaks, is a full sister to the top-class Nathaniel.

Bred for middle distances and beyond.

I'M FEELIN FINE (3YR BAY FILLY)

Trainer:	Donnacha O'Brien
Pedigree:	Almanzor – Mujabaha (Redoute's Choice)
Form:	Unraced
Optimum Trip:	1m +

Sixth foal and a half-sister to French Listed winner Magnanime and 1m 2f winner Loquito out of an unraced half-sister to 1m Listed winner Zawraq from the family of 1,000 Guineas winner Ghanaati.

Will stay a mile and should get further.

INSULATE (3YR BAY FILLY)

Trainer:	Jim Bolger
Pedigree:	Australia – Ionsai Nua (New Approach)
Form:	Unraced
Optimum Trip:	1m +

Fourth foal of an unraced dam closely related to Irish 1,000 Guineas and Yorkshire Oaks winner Pleascach from the family of Breeders' Cup winner Spain.

Sure to be well placed by her able handler and should prove effective beyond a mile.

JAVAKHETI (3YR BAY FILLY)

Trainer:	Charlie Appleby
Pedigree:	Teofilo – Lava Flow (Dalakhani)
Form:	Unraced
Optimum Trip:	1m 2f +

Fifth foal half-sister to top-class three-time Group 1 winner Pinatubo, 1m 2f winner Sundoro, UAE dirt winner Al Mureib and French middle-distance winner Antisana. Dam won a 1m 3f Listed race and comes from a good family.

Has shown plenty of ability in work at home and should live up to the family name.

LOST (3YR BAY FILLY)

Trainer:	Aidan O'Brien
Pedigree:	Frankel – Queen Cleopatra (Kingmambo)
Form:	Unraced
Optimum Trip:	1m +

Tenth foal from a very successful family, a half-sister to six winners including Australian Group 3 winner Francis Of Assisi and 1m Listed winner Look At Me. Dam, a full sister to Henrythenavigator, won at a mile and was third in the French Oaks.

Should be effective over a mile but will get further.

LUMBERJACK (3YR GREY COLT)

Trainer:	Tom Clover
Pedigree:	Mastercraftsman – Wood Chorus (Singspiel)
Form:	Unraced
Optimum Trip:	1m 4f +

Ninth foal and half-brother to five winners at trips ranging from 7f to 1m 6f. Dam was a winner and placed in Listed company. From the family of Yorkshire Cup winner Franklins Gardens and useful Group 3 winner Polar Ben.

Warranted special mention by his trainer last season and should prove effective over middle distances.

MALABU DRIVE (3YR CHESTNUT COLT)

Trainer:	Ger Lyons
Pedigree:	Frankel – Tates Creek (Rahy)
Form:	Unraced
Optimum Trip:	1m

Tenth foal and three-parts brother to GB/Australian winner Spirit Ridge and a half-brother to winners over 6f and 7f. Dam won 1m 2f Grade 1 in the States and is a half-sister to 1m 1f Grade 1 winner Sightseek.

Showed his trainer plenty of ability last season and can prove effective over a mile.

MARTINSTOWN (3YR BAY COLT)

Trainer:	Aidan O'Brien
Pedigree:	Galileo – Alive Alive Oh (Duke Of Marmalade)
Form:	Unraced
Optimum Trip:	1m 4f +

Third foal and brother to middle-distance Group 2 winner Free Wind out of a 1m 2f Listed winning half-sister to a Japanese Group 3 winner and useful 1m winner Basseterre.

Bred to suit middle distances.

MUSICAL APPROACH (3YR CHESTNUT FILLY)

Trainer:	Jim Bolger
Pedigree:	New Approach – Teo's Music (Intense Focus)
Form:	Unraced
Optimum Trip:	7f +

First foal of a winning sister to unbeaten Dewhurst Stakes winner Teofilo and a half-sister to Group 2 winner Poetic Charm.

Bred to have speed but should stay a mile.

NEL (3YR CHESTNUT FILLY)

Trainer:	Paddy Twomey
Pedigree:	Churchill – Contrary (Mark Of Esteem)
Form:	Unraced
Optimum Trip:	1m 4f

Sixth foal and a three-parts sister to a winner of five Group 1 races in Hong Kong and a half-sister to middle-distance winner Chilli Spice, 1m winner Nonno Giulio and French 1m 4f winner Duchesse.

Bred for middle distances.

NEWFOUNDLAND (3YR BAY COLT)

Trainer:	Aidan O'Brien
Pedigree:	Deep Impact – Best In The World (Galileo)
Form:	Unraced
Optimum Trip:	1m 2f +

Second foal and full brother to high-class Oaks, Irish Oaks and Yorkshire Oaks winner Snowfall out of a 1m 4f Group 3 winner Best In The World, herself a full sister to multiple Group 1 winner Found, Group 3 winner Magical Dream and Oaks third Divinely.

Superbly well bred and expected to enhance the family name.

ONE WAY (3YR BAY FILLY)

Trainer:	Donnacha O'Brien
Pedigree:	Galileo – Butterfly Cove (Storm Cat)
Form:	Unraced
Optimum Trip:	1m +

Thirteenth foal and a full sister to four winners including Irish 1,000 Guineas winner Misty For Me, 1m Group 1 winner Ballydoyle and Listed winner Twirl.

Bred to stay a mile or more.

PEROTAN (3YR BAY FILLY)

Trainer:	Aidan O'Brien
Pedigree:	Churchill – Tanaghum (Darshaan)
Form:	Unraced
Optimum Trip:	1m 4f

Twelfth foal and three-parts sister to useful performers Bangkok and Yaazy and a half-sister to seven further winners including Group 1 winner Matterhorn and 1m 6f Group 3 winner Tactic.

Comes from a very successful winning family and should do well over middle distances.

PORTHOS (3YR BAY COLT)

Trainer:	Donnacha O'Brien
Pedigree:	Galileo – Sun Shower (Indian Ridge)
Form:	Unraced
Optimum Trip:	1m +

Eleventh foal and a half-brother to seven winners including multiple Group winner Excelebration, Group 1 winner Lancaster Bomber, Group 3 winner Mull Of Killough and useful Canadian performer War Bomber.

Comes from a very successful family and should prove effective beyond a mile.

PURE DIGNITY (3YR CHESTNUT FILLY)

Trainer:	Roger Varian
Pedigree:	Dubawi – Starlet's Sister (Galileo)
Form:	Unraced
Optimum Trip:	1m 4f

€2,500,000 as a yearling and the sixth foal half-sister to high class Arc winner Sottsass, US Group 1 winner Sistercharlie and middle-distance Group 3 winner My Sister Nat.

Superbly well bred.

ROGUE ROCKET (3YR CHESTNUT GELDING)

Trainer:	Tom Clover
Pedigree:	Recorder – Eva Kant (Medicean)
Form:	Unraced
Optimum Trip:	1m 2f +

Seventh foal and a half-brother to French winners La Fibre and Kant Excell, out of an Italian sprint-winning sister to New Zealand 1m 2f Group 1 winner Turn Tide.

Already gelded but said to be useful.

SEA STONE (3YR BAY COLT)

Trainer:	Ismail Mohammed
Pedigree:	Sea The Stars – White Moonstone (Dynaformer)
Form:	Unraced
Optimum Trip:	1m +

Sixth foal and half-brother to three winners up to 1m 2f out of Group 1 Fillies' Mile winner White Moonstone.

Should stay beyond a mile.

TASHKENT (3YR BAY COLT)

Trainer:	Richard Hannon
Pedigree:	Acclamation – Colour Blue (Holy Roman Emperor)
Form:	Unraced
Optimum Trip:	6f

Second foal of winning and Listed placed half-sister to six winners including Dream The Blues, dam of 6f Group 1 winner Sioux Nation.

Bred to be speedy.

WATERVILLE (3YR BAY COLT)

Trainer:	Aidan O'Brien
Pedigree:	Camelot – Holy Moon (Hernando)
Form:	Unraced
Optimum Trip:	1m 4f

Twelfth foal and three-parts brother to Italian/French winner Magical Mystery and half-brother to 10 winners including Irish Oaks and Arc runner-up Sea Of Class and Italian Group 1 winners Final Score and Charity Line.

Dam won over 1m 4f.

Bred to stay well and reported very useful.

WHISPERING ROMANCE (3YR BAY FILLY)

Trainer:	Charlie Appleby
Pedigree:	Kingman – Sante (Dream Ahead)
Form:	Unraced
Optimum Trip:	7f +

Cost 1,450,000 guineas as a yearling and the first foal of a 7f-winning half-sister to 1m Group 2 winner Combat Zone, 1m 1f winner Scottish and 1m 5f winner Royal Empire from the family of a French Guineas winner.

Should prove effective at trips up to a mile.

WHITE CAVIAR (3YR BAY FILLY)

Trainer:	Joseph O'Brien
Pedigree:	Australia – Curious Mind (Dansili)
Form:	Unraced
Optimum Trip:	1m 4f

Second foal and full sister to St Leger winner Galileo Chrome out of a winning half-sister to 1m 3f Listed winners Michelangelo and Private Secretary.

Could be interesting over a distance of ground.

ZASHA (3YO BAY FILLY)

Trainer:	Dermot Weld
Pedigree:	Camelot – Zero Gravity (Dansili)
Form:	Unraced
Optimum Trip:	1m 4f +

Sixth foal and a half-sister to GB/US winner Vividly and Swiss jumps winner Reinvent out of a Listed middle-distance winning sister to 1m 4f Group 1 winner Zambezi Sun.

Bred to stay well.

ZERO CARBON (3YR BAY COLT)

Trainer:	Richard Hughes
Pedigree:	Acclamation – Clotilde (Dubawi)
Form:	Unraced
Optimum Trip:	7f +

Second foal of a Listed-placed, 1m winner out of a Listed-winning half-sister to useful 6f performer Kaldoun Kingdom.

Showed ability in work last season.

THE 2000 GUINEAS PREVIEW

The market for the 2022 renewal of the 2000 Guineas is dominated by horses trained by Aidan O'Brien and Charlie Appleby.

The current favourite is **Native Trail**, a son of Oasis Dream who is unbeaten in four starts. His career began in a 7f maiden at Sandown in June, where he surged up the climb to the line to beat Royal Patronage by four lengths.

That turned out to be very useful form, with the runner-up progressing later in the summer to win at Group 3 and then Group 2 level.

The feature of the winner's performance was the tenacity he showed in the final furlong. His trainer Charlie Appleby said afterwards that the colt 'had a good mind' for a Breeze-Up acquisition horse and that his work beforehand, notably with a horse that won earlier in the week, had been encouraging.

Native Trail's next race came just a month later in the 7f Group 2 Superlative Stakes at Newmarket. Once again he won the race with a late burst (he touched 21 in running on Betfair), having been keen in the early stages, getting up close home to beat the 90-rated Masekela by a short head, with the 101-rated Coventry Stakes sixth Dhabab a length and a half away in third.

Afterwards the trainer commented on the colt's strength at the finish having had concerns about the quick ground, despite his being a son of Oasis Dream whose progeny generally favour a fast surface.

Connections then gave the colt a couple of months off and he returned to action in the Group 1 National Stakes at the Curragh, where he came up against the highly vaunted Chesham Stakes winner Point Lonsdale and Group 1 Phoenix Stakes winner Ebro River.

Once again he had to be shuffled along two furlongs from home, looking held in third for a few strides, before responding to firm driving to beat Point Lonsdale by three and a half lengths – a margin that had appeared highly improbable a furlong and a half from home.

His trainer described him as 'an interesting horse to have around', adding that they had applied a cross noseband to help him concentrate as he had shown a tendency to be keen in the early stages of his races.

Just under a month later he lined up for the Group 1 Dewhurst Stakes, starting a well-supported 5/6 favourite.

Settling better this time, he travelled well in fourth just a couple of lengths off the lead before, again, appearing to become outpaced two furlongs from home. Switched right, off the rails, he moved up alongside the leader Dubawi Legend before digging deep to win going away by a couple of lengths.

After the race the trainer praised the efforts of his staff and said that once the colt met the rising ground he was never going to stop galloping. He added that he was an 'exciting Guineas horse'.

Native Trail appears to require every yard of the seven furlongs and shapes as if he will benefit from a mile. His dam is an unraced full sister to 2008 Group 1 Sprint Cup winner African Rose out of a half-sister to Distant Music, who was best at around a mile.

Having said that Native Trail's way of racing strongly suggests he is more a galloper than a colt with gears and, provided he continues to settle, a stiff mile and perhaps a little further should be within range.

This colt has class and a tenacious will to win. He is a very likeable individual and his position at the head of the Guineas market is thoroughly warranted.

The feeling that I gleaned from those close to the yard is that stable companion **Coroebus** was, at one stage, considered his equal if not a little better.

The son of Dubawi ended the campaign rated 7lbs inferior to Native Trail, but his three runs – all over a mile – left a lasting impression.

His campaign started at Newmarket in August when he drew clear to beat subsequent winner Saga by a length and a quarter, with the third, fourth, fifth and sixth going on to win shortly afterwards.

About six weeks later he turned up for the Group 2 Royal Lodge Stakes at Newmarket, meeting Royal Patronage and Masekela, who had both chased home Native Trail earlier in the season.

Tracking Royal Patronage early on, he moved smoothly into the lead four furlongs from home and then found an impressive turn of foot approaching the two-furlong marker to pull four lengths clear, looking sure to win.

It was then that Royal Patronage began to stay on again and he caught the leader two strides from home to win by a neck. The trainer said afterwards that Coroebus had got 'a little lonely in front' and had been picked off by a horse who knew more about the game.

It was the general consensus afterwards that Coroebus was the best horse in the field and that he would benefit from being held up for longer when he next appeared.

That came in the Group 3 Autumn Stakes in October, where he was tucked away last in the nearside bunch. Approaching the two-furlong marker he moved up alongside his rivals and found a change of gear that got him home two lengths clear of Imperial

Fighter who, a fortnight later, ran well in the Group 1 Futurity Stakes at Doncaster.

Charlie Appleby said afterwards that the colt had 'taken his jockey by surprise' with the acceleration he had shown the time before, and it was the case again here, adding that he was 'doing stuff on the gallops in the spring that he shouldn't have been given his size'.

The trainer said the Craven and the Guineas would be the plan.

Coroebus, whose three starts were over a mile, has a little more stamina in his pedigree than Native Trail. His dam, a 7f winner, is a half-sister to Thunder Snow, a winner of four Group/Grade 1 races up to 1m 2f including the Dubai World Cup twice, and other winners at a mile.

The BHA assessor has rated Native Trail 7lbs superior to Coroebus and a tenuous line through Royal Patronage suggests that is right.

The question, regarding the 2000 Guineas, is whether connections will pitch the two colts against each other? On the one hand Coroebus is proven over the trip and has a potent turn of foot, while Native Trail is more a galloper who should stay, and possibly improve, over the mile.

Perhaps it will depend on how the two colts shape up this spring. I would be surprised if they were to both line up for the Craven, let alone the Guineas, and there are obviously other options in Ireland and France.

Aidan O'Brien has a 'buzz horse' every year and the colt to whom that title fell last year was **Luxembourg**, a son of Camelot out of a half-sister to middle-distance winners from the family of Group 3 Glorious Stakes and hurdle winner Forgotten Voice.

It is hard to crab a colt that ended the season unbeaten in three starts, the final one coming in the Group 1 Futurity Stakes at Doncaster, but this is not an easy horse to warm to.

His debut came in a median sires race at Killarney in July, where he responded to quiet urgings from the saddle to beat Tuwaiq, who ended the season rated 102.

A couple of months later he met the runner-up again in the Group 2 Beresford Stakes at the Curragh, settled last of five before being switched two furlongs from home and then producing an instant turn of foot which saw him pass the post four and three-quarter lengths clear of the second.

His third appearance came in the Group 1 Futurity Stakes at Doncaster, where he encountered soft ground for the first time. On this occasion he required firmer handling to take the lead, but the turn of foot we had seen at the Curragh was less evident as he held on to beat a bunch for second by one and three-quarter lengths.

Afterwards the trainer said his colt 'would have preferred a stronger gallop' and was 'babyish in front'. Earlier in the season the experienced and astute Seamie Heffernan had commented on how smart the colt is at home, but that he doesn't show it until you 'press the button'.

The feature that worries me about this colt is his ungainly head carriage.

In fairness it was less obvious on his final start, and there is no denying he displayed a scintillating turn of foot at the Curragh, but a line through Bayside Boy suggests Native Trail may just have the edge – albeit a narrow one – and the standard of Ballydoyle juveniles last season fell short of previous years.

Furthermore, the colt has more stamina in his pedigree than speed and he may be caught out over a mile. He is more likely to stay a mile and a half than the two Godolphin colts, for whom the Derby is unlikely to be a consideration, and a good run at Newmarket may set him up for Epsom.

However the trainer has said that Luxembourg was 'always the horse' and from the time he went to his maiden at Killarney they knew he was 'very good'.

We have, of course, heard this before, but Aidan O'Brien calls things as he sees them and I have no doubt that at this time Luxembourg is their pick.

Stable companion **Point Lonsdale** was the Ballydoyle 'banker' at Royal Ascot, where he landed the odds in the Chesham Stakes by half a length from the promising Reach For The Moon.

That came on the back of a workmanlike wide-margin success in a 7f maiden at the Curragh. Following his Royal Ascot victory he landed the Group 3 Tyros Stakes at Leopardstown, striding clear to win by three lengths from Maritime Wings, before beating the same horse by a little further in a Group 2 at the Curragh.

The son of Australia lost his unbeaten record on his fifth and final start when totally outpointed by Native Trail in the Group 1 National Stakes back at the Curragh. Looking at this race it's difficult to imagine him reversing the form with the winner unless, of course, he improves significantly for the step up to a mile.

Regarding that prospect, and based on his pedigree, there is a very good chance that he could improve for the longer trip. His sire Australia won the Derby and Irish Derby while he is a full brother to Group 1 1m 4f winner Broome and a half-brother to other winners including Horseshoe Bay.

However, judging by the chatter from Ballydoyle, Luxembourg is rated the better of the two colts – which given their style of racing does not come as any surprise. However, Point Lonsdale is a thoroughly genuine galloper with, from what I've seen, a maturity beyond his years. His trainer says that he is a 'very brave horse' whose head goes 'right down to the ground'.

Point Lonsdale could be just the type his trainer likes to keep busy, perhaps following something akin to the programme he has set for other great names from the past.

Moving down the list to the horses quoted in double figures we come to **Modern Games**, a son of Dubawi trained by Charlie Appleby.

Following a relatively low-key start to his career at Haydock in July, when he ran fifth of 10 beaten 11 lengths, he quickened to beat Saga – who next time ran second to Coroebus – by two lengths in a 7f maiden at Newmarket.

The following month he found Cresta too smart for him at Leicester, despite looking the winner for much of the race, before winning a 7f nursery off 90 with plenty in hand at Doncaster.

He then built on that when winning the Group 3 Tattersalls Stakes at Newmarket, with Leicester conqueror Cresta four lengths back in fourth, before his sixth and final start in the Grade 1 Breeders' Cup Juvenile Turf at Del Mar, where he powered clear, head bowed low, having hung wide round the home turn to win pulling clear by a length and a half.

This was a far cry from the colt we saw beaten so far on his debut at Haydock four months earlier and he appeals as the ideal type to tackle an international programme. As for his optimum trip, his half-brothers won up to seven furlongs and his dam is related to milers.

To the eye Modern Games looks likely to stay ten furlongs, especially on the quick ground that suited him so well last season. Described by his handler as a 'neat little horse', he would apparently struggle to keep tabs with Native Trail in their work at home, but there is no denying his tenacity and his trackcraft.

Modern Games may not be aimed at the Guineas but he could be one to keep in mind for a top prize in the height of summer. Do not underestimate him.

Moving on in the market we come next to **Perfect Power**, the colt most likely from the exposed crop to trouble the might of the two great behemoths of Godolphin and Ballydoyle.

This son of Group 2 winner Ardad, who stands at Overbury Stud for a relatively modest £12,500, won four of his six starts including the Norfolk Stakes and on his fifth and sixth outings, the Prix Morny and the Middle Park Stakes at Newmarket.

The feature of his victories has been his turn of foot. That first became evident in his maiden at Hamilton, albeit at a lowly level, but he then did the same at Royal Ascot, coming from off the pace.

We saw the same burst of speed at Deauville and Newmarket, on the latter occasion making very good late headway from an unfavourable position.

Between times he was probably unfortunate not to win the Richmond Stakes at Goodwood, never getting a clear run and finishing full of running.

The first impression from his form is that he will prove best suited to trips short of a mile. This is, though, not supported by his pedigree. His dam won at 1m 2f and is a half-sister to a black type-placed winner over the same trip from the family of Arc winner Sagamix.

Trainer Richard Fahey says the colt had a busy campaign last summer but 'spends most of his time asleep' and he has a 'super mind'.

I see no reason why he should not be tried at a mile, as he can always revert to sprinting afterwards if it doesn't work out. He is a dual Group 1 winner, rated on the same mark as Coroebus, and he has as good a turn of foot as anything in the field.

It will be intriguing to learn what connections have in store for him.

Angel Bleu, a son of Dark Angel trained by Ralph Beckett, is also rated on 115 but his fondness for soft ground suggests his target is more likely to be the Poule d'Essai des Poulains at Paris-Longchamp.

There was no hint of his future dual Group 1 successes when he went down by five lengths on his debut in a 5f novice contest at Leicester in early April, but he then won his next two starts, wasn't beaten far by Berkshire Shadow in the Coventry Stakes and then reversed the form with that winner on his preferred softer ground in the Group 2 Vintage Stakes at Goodwood.

Frankie Dettori was seen at his best on the colt's last two starts, coming from off the pace to win the Prix Jean-Luc Lagardere from Noble Truth and Ancient Rome at Longchamp in October and then later that month, under a ride bordering on arrogance, he beat Ancient Rome by a head in the Group 1 Criterium International at Saint-Cloud.

Angel Bleu clearly stays a mile well, and he is especially suited to testing ground. As to getting further, he is the first foal of a full sister to top-class middle-distance winner Highland Reel and 1m 4f Group 2 winner Idaho, so ten furlongs should not present a problem.

Ralph Beckett says the colt is a 'privilege to be involved with' and that horses like him do not come his way very often. France looks to be his spring target, but he could be one to keep in mind for the richly endowed autumn prizes in the mud. One thing we can rely on is that his handler will place him to optimum advantage.

Roger Varian's **Bayside Boy** could become popular at 25/1 given the high esteem in which he is held by his talented handler.

In essence he has fallen a little short of the best of his contemporaries, beaten by Masekela at Newbury in August, by Native Trail in the Dewhurst and then by Luxembourg in the Group 1 Futurity at Doncaster.

His trainer points out that he did not get a clear run when he needed it at Doncaster and, in his defence, he is a colt that needs to wind up and build momentum rather than one who can deliver an instant change of gear.

The trouble is that he is just lacking an edge. He is a half-brother to the versatile Forest Ranger and a winner over a mile and a half in France, so he may improve for an extra quarter-mile.

In my view he is a tough, reliable sort who will appreciate a stiff ten furlongs. His trainer hopes to have him ready for the Guineas and he could be the type to stay on up the hill and finish in the first four. A little cut underfoot would help his cause.

Dewhurst runner-up **Dubawi Legend**, a half-brother to 1m 4f Listed winner Golden Pass, warrants respect despite his final effort when down the field behind Modern Games at Del Mar. He can be keen and needs to relax if he is to realise his potential.

Jane Chapple-Hyam was not entertaining an angel unawares when saddling **Claymore** to make a winning debut in a 7f novice stakes at Newmarket in late October.

The son of New Bay, who had been supported at long odds the night before, made all to beat Noble Order by four lengths but that colt, trained by Charlie Appleby, ended his season on 87 and is not rated in the same league as the two at the head of this market.

Having said that connections have big plans for Claymore, who looks exceptionally well bought at just £10,000 as a Breeze-Up consignation.

Greater things were expected of **Glounthaune** when he ran in the Dewhurst, finishing sixth, and he was then less convincing than his trainer Aidan O'Brien had hoped when he beat Pennine Hills by half a length in a Group 3 at Leopardstown. That was a messy affair but there was just the hint of a turn of foot and he is probably capable of nicking a decent race, probably beyond a mile.

Star Of India was described as 'a grand staying type' by Seamie Heffernan after landing a 7f maiden at Leopardstown in October. His distaff side is actually more speed biased but I discerned a very willing attitude in the way this colt went about his business.

The form has subsequently been let down by the third, but connections will probably sneak a Group race or two out of him. The trainer has said they may aim him at the French Classics.

River Thames stayed on in pleasing fashion to beat stable companion Changingoftheguard in a 1m maiden at Punchestown in September, but the runner-up is rated just 87 and that falls way short of the requisite level.

He may also be aimed at France.

King Of Bavaria, a son of No Nay Never, was rated potential Royal Ascot material by Aidan O'Brien after he won a Naas maiden in May but he then suffered a minor setback. He reappeared back there in a nursery in October, which he won in heavy ground from a mark of 95.

That was a gutsy effort in the ground, leading to a 10lbs rise to 105. He may start off in a Guineas trial.

Joseph O'Brien will have hopes for recent acquisition **Hannibal Barca**, who won a novice event for Brian Meehan at Salisbury in September before running a very creditable fourth, beaten two lengths, in the Futurity.

His former trainer was talking of him running in the Craven, convinced he had Group 1 potential for the future, and it will be interesting to learn if his new handler harbours similar ambitions. If he settles he should stay beyond a mile.

Andrew Balding's **Hoo Ya Mal**, by Territories out of a Montjeu mare, should also stay beyond a mile. Rated on 105, he needs to improve from his Listed second at Doncaster in September.

David Simcock and the Never Say Die partnership should have some fun with **Light Infantry**. The son of Fast Company beat subsequent triple winner High Velocity by a wide margin on his Yarmouth debut in September and then ground out a hard-fought success in the Group 3 Horris Hill Stakes at Newbury.

That form earned him a mark of 107, but he was still very green at Newbury – hanging right close home – and he will be given his chance in an early trial. He comes from a family of milers.

Andre Fabre's **Rebel Path**, a 6f winner at Deauville in August, is not bred for a mile. Godolphin have likelier contenders higher up the order.

The aforementioned **Royal Patronage** may take his chance at Newmarket but his future lies over middle distances. The first foal of the Aga Khan-owned middle-distance winner Shaloushka, he is from the family of Irish Derby third Shalapour and Derby and Irish Derby winner Shahrastani.

He will be competitively campaigned by Charlie and Mark Johnston and could be the type to go close in the King Edward VII Stakes at Royal Ascot.

The Guineas and Derby entries for the Del Mar Breeders' Cup runner-up **Tiz The Bomb**, a winner in March of a conditions race at Turfway Park, are highly ambitious but nonetheless intriguing.

Kevin Ryan is nobody's fool so we need to take notice when he describes Haydock Listed winner **Triple Time** as a Guineas horse.

The son of Frankel maintained a strong gallop to beat Hafit but the runner-up is trained by Charlie Appleby, so he will have the measure of the form. Before that he had stormed clear to win a 1m novice stakes in soft ground effortlessly by nine and a half lengths from a colt now rated on 84.

Triple Time, who is bred to stay further than a mile, has won on both soft and fast ground. He looks tough and, knowing his owner's enthusiasm for pitching his horses in at a high level, I expect him to earn black type at some point.

Ger Lyons will win something decent with **Atomic Jones**, a big colt with a large frame to fill. The son of Wootton Bassett won both his starts last season, the second by a head from Stone Age in a 1m Group 2 at Leopardstown in September. He showed great tenacity to get up close home there and his trainer expects him to thrive as he progresses through the season. He should stay a mile and a quarter, possibly further.

The same trainer has another Group-class performer with **Dr Zempf**, who chased home Ebro River in the Group 1 Phoenix Stakes at the Curragh in August before finishing two and three-quarter lengths behind Perfect Power in the Middle Park Stakes at Newmarket.

The son of Dark Angel is related to performers who were are at their most effective at trips short of a mile, but he battled on well to beat The Acropolis in a 7f Listed race at Leopardstown in April and Newmarket was mentioned afterwards by the trainer.

It is probably significant that William Haggas has made just one entry for the race from his classy crop of three-year-olds.

Al Mubhir won a 7f maiden at Newmarket in October on his only start, responding to strong driving to get up close home to beat subsequent winner Filistine by a length.

The third horse has since let down the form but the trainer does not make frivolous entries so it is fair to assume he holds this son of Frankel in high esteem. There is middle-distance blood on the bottom line of his pedigree so he may stay beyond a mile.

Jim Bolger can never be discounted at this level and he has made an entry for **Boundless Ocean**, who was beaten in each of his three starts – over the space of nine days – last season. Having said that, he was not disgraced on the second and third occasions in Group 3 company at Leopardstown.

His third start was over nine furlongs and as a full brother to two winners over hurdles he looks likely in time to prove effective over a mile and a quarter or more. However, his first run this season was back over 7f in late March at the Curragh, starting a shade of odds-on, and he made a bold effort to make all but was just touched off on the line by debutant Malex.

Wexford Native, a son of Teofilo, impressed on his racecourse debut in a 1m maiden at Navan in March. That was a very good effort from his high draw in stall 21 but the Guineas may come too soon for him.

The trainer has also entered the unraced **Frazil**, a full brother to his Guineas winner Poetic Flare.

James Ferguson has charge of the useful **El Bodegon**, a son of Kodiac who progressed from winning a 7f novice stakes in heavy ground at Sandown in July to landing a 1m 1f Group 3 at Chantilly in September, followed by the 1m 2f Criterium de Saint-Cloud just under a month later.

The colt, who has a compact build, made all at Saint-Cloud, staying on dourly in the testing ground to beat the four-race maiden Stone Age, who ended the season on a rating of 109. The third was Newmarket Group 3 winner Goldspur, trained by Charlie Appleby, with the consistent Buckaroo back in fourth.

This is a decent level of form, albeit about 10lbs below the standard required to win a Guineas, but El Bodegon's future is likely to be over further than a mile. He is already a Group 1 winner over ten furlongs and he is a half-brother to a middle-distance winner and a winner over hurdles.

Watch for him in the autumn mud.

Saga, a grey son of Invincible Spirit and the ninth foal of a Group 3-winning daughter of Machiavellian, came up against Modern Games and Coroebus on his first two starts. He then made all to comfortably win a 7f maiden at Ascot, holding subsequent winner Koy Koy with something to spare.

Owned by the Queen, he looks capable of earning black type at some point. His opening mark of 92 offers a platform on which to build.

French handler Fabrice Chappet has entered unbeaten three-times winner **Topgear** for the Guineas.

The son of Wootton Bassett won twice at Deauville in August before beating Best Flying narrowly in the Group 3 Prix Eclipse at Chantilly in September. He is related to milers so the trip should not present any problem. He is, though, probably more likely to stay in France.

A Guineas entry for **Tylos** suggests that Simon and Ed Crisford should be able to exploit the colt's opening mark of 87.

Martyn Meade produces a good horse most years and **Zechariah**, a winner at Sandown and Newbury, can progress through the season. There was much to like about the way he kept up his gallop on the latter occasion.

Eydon, a son of Olden Times trained by Roger Varian, has shaped well in finishing third and second in two 1m maidens at Newcastle this winter. He would not carry an entry here unless his trainer held out hopes for him.

Roger Teal, who does so well with the stock that comes his way, should have plenty of fun with Newbury runner-up **My Mate Ted** as should Richard Hannon with **Razzle Dazzle**, who is better than he looked when sixth on his final start at Doncaster. The trainer also has **Gisburn**, who put up a good time when winning a Newbury maiden in May and ended the season with a nursery success off 90.

William Knight has entered **Checkandchallenge**, who got up in the last stride to beat a fair performer in his sole start at Wolverhampton.

David Loughnane is moving up the ranks and he thinks highly of **Kingmax**, who won a 1m novice stakes at Kempton very easily in March, having run second twice last season with Roger Varian. He is bred to stay further than a mile and, rated on 86, is probably ahead of his mark.

Finally, keep on the right side of **New Energy**.

Sheila Lavery's son of New Bay was quietly supported when making a winning debut in a 7f maiden at the Curragh in September and it was disappointing to see him well held in a Group 3 the following month at Leopardstown.

He is probably a little better than he looked when third to Dr Zempf in the Guineas Trial at Leopardstown in April.

The colt is related to middle-distance winners and he could be the sort to pop up somewhere at a good price, possibly beyond a mile.

Conclusion

At the time of writing it seems likely that Charlie Appleby will run both Native Trail and Coroebus, while Aidan O'Brien has left nobody in any doubt that Luxembourg is his primary candidate. He could, though, be joined by Point Lonsdale.

If the four colts turn up it is hard to imagine anything else getting a look in. Of the two Godolphin colts I prefer Coroebus, proven over the mile and with a better turn of foot than his stable companion.

I struggle to warm to Luxembourg – though respecting the high esteem in which he is held by his trainer – while Point Lonsdale's commendable attitude may not be sufficient to bridge the National Stakes deficit with Native Trail.

Perfect Power possibly has the best turn of foot in the field but he is not yet a confirmed runner and this looks as if it's going to be a very high-class Guineas.

As you will have gathered I have a great fondness for Bayside Boy. The colt has run close to Native Trail and Luxembourg but he is a grinder, just a few pounds behind the best. A winter's development may have helped but he may need an extra quarter-mile to beat the best. I do, though, like him.

Triple Time warrants a mention but it is hard to see beyond the top four – five if you include Perfect Power.

I like Coroebus and Point Lonsdale, both each-way, at 5/1 and 10/1 respectively. Bayside Boy, at 25/1, is worth a saver.

THE OAKS PREVIEW

Connections will be keen to let **Inspiral** take her chance here if everything goes well in the Guineas.

The daughter of Frankel can be keen but she soon settles down and has a style of racing which augurs well for a step up in trip. Her three-parts sister Astrologer won over an extended 7f but was never tried beyond a mile, while her half-sister Celestran won over 1m 2f and was runner-up over 1m 4f despite being a free-running sort.

Inspiral's dam stayed an extended 1m 2f when fourth in the Group 2 Middleton Stakes at York, having been runner-up a year earlier in the 1000 Guineas.

It's a close call regarding this trip for Inspiral. Much will depend on how she has matured through the winter and if she settles better, but taking everything into account I expect her to stay.

Tuesday, a short-head runner-up to subsequent Group 1 Moyglare Stud Stakes winner Discoveries at the Curragh in June, has progressed to the top of the market following her win in a 1m maiden contest at Naas in March.

This daughter of Galileo is a full sister to Oaks winner Minding and Irish 1,000 Guineas winner Empress Josephine out of dual Group 1 Coronation Stakes and Matron Stakes winner Lillie Langtry.

Tuesday should stay the Oaks trip but her form at this stage leaves her something to find.

Agave, unbeaten in three starts for Andre Fabre, has won a 1m 2f Listed race and then last time the Group 3 Prix Penelope over an extended 1m 2f, both this spring at Saint-Cloud.

She is by Dubawi out of a daughter of Champs Elysees who won over 1m 7f and comes from the family of Enable. She is bred to relish the mile and a half.

So, too, is Joseph O'Brien's Leopardstown 1m 2f maiden winner **Above The Curve**, a daughter of American Pharoah out of an unraced daughter of Galileo.

Aidan O'Brien has entered 13 fillies for the race.

Concert Hall finished four and a quarter lengths behind Inspiral in the Group 1 Fillies' Mile last October. By Dubawi out of Oaks winner Was, she should have no problem with the trip.

Stable companion **History**, who cost 2,800,000gns as a yearling, is the first foal of 1m winner Prize Exhibit, a daughter of Showcasing. She may be best at a mile and 1m 2f.

Toy, a full sister to 2000 Guineas winner Gleneagles, may also be best at trips up to 1m 2f.

The unraced **Champagne**, a full sister to seven winners including Arc winner Found and to the dam of Snowfall, has a middle-distance pedigree.

So, too, has the unraced **Over The Rainbow**. She is by Dubawi and the first foal of Group 1 Yorkshire Oaks winner Seventh Heaven.

Perotan, by Churchill and a three-parts sister to Bangkok and other winners over middle distances, is also worth bearing in mind.

Aidan O'Brien has high hopes for **Only**, by Deep Impact and the first foal of four-time Group 1 winner Winter. She shaped well when runner-up to stable companion Lullaby at Leopardstown in April.

Galway winner **The Algarve** is out of Irish Oaks and 1,000 Guineas winner Imagine, dam of 10 winners including Group 1 winner Van Gogh. She should stay.

There is better to come from **Emily Dickinson**, who has run well in two maidens at Leopardstown. Black type beckons for her.

Eclat De Lumiere won a 7f maiden at the Curragh for Dermot Weld last August. She is by Sea The Stars and a full sister to 1m 4f winner Listen In and a half-sister to Dominant, who won three times over 1m 4f including the Group 1 Hong Kong Vase at Sha Tin. She should stay.

Mise En Scene makes some appeal.

The daughter of Siyouni, who is trained by James Ferguson, is a half-sister to a winner at 1m 3f out of an unraced half-sister to 1000 Guineas winner Speciosa, and a US Grade 3 winner over 1m 4f, from the family of Grade 1 middle-distance winner Pride.

She won her first two starts, both over 7f, landing a Group 3 at Goodwood on the second occasion and then stayed on steadily when fourth to Inspiral in the Fillies' Mile. She wasn't disgraced on her final outing when beaten four and a quarter lengths in the Breeders' Cup at Del Mar.

Ed Walker has charge of **Kawida**, a daughter of Sir Percy out of a dam by Archipenko. She eventually got the better of Flash Betty in a 1m Listed race at Newmarket in October, looking an out-and-out stayer. She is one for extreme trips.

Kawida is owned by Kirsten Rausing, who also has **Ching Shih** with David Simcock.

I have written very favourably about this daughter of Lope De Vega elsewhere. She impressed in her novice at Newbury in October and could hardly have a stronger staying pedigree.

She is a half-sister to 1m 4f Listed winner Oriental Mystique out of Group 1 Ascot Fillies & Mares Stakes winner Madame Chiang. At 50/1 she makes some appeal.

I nominated John Gosden's Taghrooda for this race back in 2013 having won a maiden and on the strength of her strong middle-distance pedigree.

Morning Poem, who won a 1m novice stakes at Kempton in November, has a similar profile.

John and Thady Gosden's daughter of Kingman may not have beaten much – the third is rated 76 – but she came from a long way back and produced a useful turn of foot to get up close home.

Her dam won a 1m 6f Listed race and is a full sister to a winner over 1m 4f from the family of an Oaks third.

She can be backed at 40/1 as I write and I suggest you watch for her being entered for a trial.

Stable companion **Emily Upjohn** displayed battling qualities when winning over an extended 1m 1f at Wolverhampton in November.

The unraced **Emotion**, by Frankel out of a 2m 4f Prix du Cadran winner, is bred to stay long distances. She is one to keep an eye on.

Hugo Palmer's Chelmsford novice winner **Arion** is bred to stay but needs to settle better.

Cet Horizon, a daughter of Iffraaj trained by William Haggas, made all to win over an extended mile at Nottingham in October. Her dam won beyond a mile and a half and comes from a family chock-full of middle-distance blood.

She is one to note over a distance of ground.

The trainer has made an entry for the unraced **Pawapuri**, a daughter of the owner's Golden Horn and a half-sister to winners up to an extended 1m 3f. The dam is a full sister to 2000 Guineas winner Footstepsinthesand and she would not be entered here without good reason.

Perfect Alibi, from the same yard and owned by The Queen, is by Le Havre and the first foal of 1m 6f winner Daphne from the family of Highland Glen, Bold Sniper and Oaks runner-up Flight Of Fancy.

This beautifully bred filly has a future over middle distances.

The trainer has also entered **Remembering**, a daughter of Frankel, but she has bundles of speed on her distaff side and is a doubtful stayer in my view.

He has also made an entry for **Tamilla**, who showed some promise at Nottingham and Wolverhampton.

Ralph Beckett has an excellent record with his middle-distance fillies.

Luna Dorada stayed on well to beat Gin O'Clock in a 1m novice stakes at York on her sole start. The daughter of Golden Horn is a half-sister to a winner over hurdles from the family of St Leger winner Brian Boru and Derby and Arc winner Workforce. She looks sure to thrive over a trip.

The trainer also has charge of Doncaster maiden winner **Moon De Vega**, rated 80 after her three runs and out of a 1m 3f winner. She is also bred to stay.

Stable companion **Suspicious**, a winner of her sole start at Doncaster in August, is a half-sister to a 1m 4f winner. She beat subsequent winner Beautiful Secret, now rated on 84.

Paddy Twomey should have a good season with **Show Of Stars**.

The daughter of Showcasing comfortably won a 1m maiden at Dundalk in November, building on the promise she had shown on her debut, and this half-sister to a 1m 6f winner from the family of Elusive Pimpernel should earn black type at some stage.

Roger Varian can win races with **Divine Jewel**, a daughter of Frankel out of the useful Group 2 winner Agnes Stewart from a middle-distance family. She shaped well when placed in her two starts at Nottingham and Redcar.

He has a more obvious contender with **Peripatetic**, a daughter of Ulysses who won a 1m maiden at Newcastle in October.

Eve Johnson Houghton will win races with twice-raced **Suzy's Shoes**, but this looks ambitious.

Finally, **Life Of Dreams** looks interesting. Charlie Appleby's daughter of Dubawi is the first foal of seven-race winner Endless Time, who won the Group 2 Lancashire Oaks over 1m 4f and a Group 3 at Goodwood over 1m 6f.

She should flourish over a distance of ground.

Conclusion

Inspiral is the clear pick on form and this will probably be her target if she runs well in the Guineas.

The Oaks, though, can be won by a filly from the maiden ranks and those that interest me are Morning Poem and Ching Shih, while from the unraced crop I like the pedigrees of Champagne, Emotion, Life Of Dreams, Over The Rainbow, Perotan and Perfect Alibi.

Mise En Scene and Luna Dorada will win races at a decent level but the two I suggest, at this time, are Morning Poem and Ching Shih.

THE DERBY PREVIEW

Many of the colts that appear in the early market for the 2022 Cazoo Derby are featured in my 2000 Guineas preview, so I will be focusing on their stamina credentials rather than their form.

Top of the market, at odds ranging from 5/2 to 4/1, is the unbeaten **Luxembourg** who ended the season with a somewhat unconvincing victory in the Group 1 Futurity Stakes at Doncaster.

It's probably safe to assume that the son of Camelot was the pick of Aidan O'Brien's crop of two-year-olds despite not convincing everyone with his style of racing. Regarding his stamina, he is a half-brother to extended 1m 2f Group 2 Mooresbridge Stakes winner Leo De Fury, who won at a modest level over 1m 4f, and 1m 4f maiden winner Lady Dahlia.

His dam is a full sister to 1m 4f Group 3 Glorious Stakes winner Forgotten Voice so I think, given his relaxed way of racing, that he will stay a mile and a half. Furthermore, if he can conserve his energy and reproduce the turn of foot we witnessed in the Beresford Stakes he could prove a very effective performer over middle distances.

Point Lonsdale could not live with Native Trail in the Group 1 National Stakes at the Curragh but were the two to meet over a mile and a quarter or more the result could be reversed.

The son of Australia is a full brother to 1m 4f Group 1 Grand Prix de Saint-Cloud winner Broome and a half-brother to five other winners including one over a mile and a half. It should be noted that his dam, by the sprinter Acclamation, won twice over 5f for Richard Hannon but Point Lonsdale looks like a galloper and the trainer is never afraid to tackle Epsom mob-handed.

Native Trail digs deep and does his best work at the end of his races but he is by the sprinter Oasis Dream out of a distaff side packed with speed and miling blood. There is a chance that if he were to win the Guineas, connections may be tempted to have a crack at Epsom, but his chance of staying is remote.

Stable companion **Coroebus** has, in my view, the stronger credentials for a mile and a half. Although he probably has a more instant change of gear than Native Trail, his sire Dubawi is a far stronger influence for stamina than Oasis Dream and his dam is a half-sister to the dual Dubai World Cup 1m 2f winner Thunder Snow.

An impressive work horse at home, it would not surprise me to see Coroebus aimed at the Derby provided his spring programme went according to plan.

Moving away from the Godolphin and Ballydoyle yards, this would be an appropriate year for the Queen to own a Derby winner.

I will never forget the look of frustration on Ryan Moore's face when he just failed to get Carlton House home in 2011 and the Queen has a very strong contender this year with **Reach For The Moon**.

The son of Sea The Stars, who is trained by John Gosden, has a rock-solid middle-distance pedigree.

His full brother Chalk Stream won three times in handicap company over a mile and a half and his half-brother Invictus Prince was placed many times over the same trip. The dam Golden Stream won at 7f and is a full sister to Oaks runner-up Flight Of Fancy out of Phantom Gold, a Group 2 winner of the extended 1m 5f Geoffrey Freer Stakes.

Given the depth of stamina in the colt's pedigree he did well to show such useful form over seven furlongs.

A promising debut, when he chased home New Science, was followed by a gutsy effort in the Chesham Stakes, where he was soon up with the pace and looking sure to win until running green and just getting outstayed close home by Point Lonsdale, with former conqueror New Science ten and three-quarter lengths back in seventh.

The colt had his sights lowered just under a month later when he won a 7f novice stakes at Newbury by four lengths from Harrow, who ended his season on a mark of 103.

The following month Reach For The Moon went to Sandown for the Group 3 Solario Stakes. Racing keenly on the outside of the field, he turned for home in fourth before producing a turn of foot to go clear of the 103-rated Great Max, winning by four lengths.

The colt's final start came in the Group 2 Champagne Stakes at Doncaster where, again, he was quite keen from the outset. On this occasion he was unable to come away as he had done at Sandown and was caught close home by Bayside Boy, who prevailed by a head at the line.

Afterwards the trainer attributed the colt's defeat to the ground, which he described as 'dead'. Frankie Dettori added that the colt never gave him the same feel as at Sandown.

The colt would have run again, with the Dewhurst a possible target, but he met with a setback which kept him off the track for the remainder of the season.

Reach For The Moon's form falls a few pounds below the market leaders – he has been beaten in a Group 2 – but he could not be in better hands and we can have no doubt that in this most special of years for the owner the Derby will be the main target.

El Bodegon is already a Group 1 winner over 1m 2f and he looks sure to stay, with St Leger winner Brian Boru in his bottom line and his full brother Best Solution a winner over a mile and a half.

James Ferguson will be keen to aim high with this colt, but his best form last season was in the mud and those conditions are unlikely to prevail at Epsom.

Walk Of Stars is quoted in some lists at 25/1.

Charlie Appleby's son of Dubawi shaped with promise when third in a 1m novice stakes at Newmarket in October and a fortnight later he made all to win over an extended mile in a maiden at Nottingham.

He took a while to assert himself on that occasion but he is a half-brother to French 1m 5f winner Moon Shimmer from the family of Nathaniel and a winner over an extended 1m 6f.

Walk Of Stars is hard to assess but he could be one to keep in mind for the St Leger.

I have written favourably about **Bayside Boy** in the 2000 Guineas Preview.

Roger Varian's son of New Bay beat Reach For The Moon in the Champagne Stakes at Doncaster and then ran second to Native Trail and Luxembourg in the Dewhurst and Futurity. He mixed it with the season's top colts and he has a half-brother who stayed a mile and a half.

Bayside Boy appeals as the sort of colt who will consistently produce his form, at a value price and at the highest level. At 33/1 in a place for the Derby he represents fair each-way value.

Dermot Weld thinks highly of **Duke De Sessa** but the son of Lope De Vega was found out at Group 1 level in the National Stakes and he will need to find over a stone's improvement for the step up in trip.

He shaped well when third on his return but the Irish Guineas looks a more suitable target.

One horse who is definitely bred for the Derby trip is **Hannibal Barca**, a son of Zoffany and a three-parts brother to Australian 1m 6f winner Fledged.

He has joined Joseph O'Brien from Brian Meehan having been last seen running fourth to Luxembourg in the Group 1 Futurity. He may have the Irish Derby as his target but rated on 111 he doesn't need to improve much to be competitive at the highest level.

Mark and Charlie Johnston are likely to keep **Royal Patronage** busy. The first foal of French middle-distance winner Shaloushka is closely related to Derby winner Shahrastani so looks sure to thrive over the Derby trip.

He can be forgiven his closing effort in the Futurity as he was struck into but his earlier form, when he beat Coroebus, reads very well.

Sir Michael Stoute does not make frivolous entries so we need to respect **Desert Crown**, who won an extended 1m maiden at Nottingham by five and a half lengths last November. The runner-up is now rated on 80, which puts the winner in the low 90s, but he was doing his best work in the final furlong and will probably prove a Group-class performer.

There are mixed messages from his pedigree regarding his trip, but he will definitely stay a mile and a quarter.

The trainer has also made a Derby entry for **Migdam**, a son of Prix Jean Prat winner Zelzal and a half-brother to middle-distance Listed winner Katara out of a strong German family.

This colt won a couple of novice stakes at Kempton in September, carrying his head a little high on the first occasion, but he knew more about the game on his final start. A mark of 89 reflects the gulf between him and the best of his generation, but he is in the right hands to make up the leeway.

Goldspur, by Dubawi out of a middle-distance-winning sister to a 2m winner, will relish a mile and a half. The Godolphin colt shaped well when third to El Bodegon in that Group 1 at Saint-Cloud in October, and he may be one to keep in mind for the St Leger.

Hafit, beaten a neck by Goldspur at Newmarket, can improve for middle distances. He should develop into a useful type, probably just short of the top level.

One of the yard's most interesting prospects is **New London**.

The son of Dubawi needed plenty of cajoling to win a 1m 2f maiden at Newmarket in October, looking well held entering the closing stages until finding the reserves to surge past Soul Stopper in the dying strides.

The runner-up has subsequently let the form down but there has been early market interest in New London on the strength of good work at home.

This dour galloper is from the family of Arc winner Waldgeist and St Leger winner Masked Marvel, and the Doncaster Classic may also be a possible target for him.

Ruling Dynasty, an unraced three-parts brother to the gutsy Old Persian, and related to other middle-distance performers, is sure to stay well.

Saeed Bin Suroor has the unraced **Return To Dubai**, by Ribchester, **White Wolf** and **Wild Tiger** to look forward to.

We didn't see **Sonny Liston**, trained by Charlie Hills, again after his winning debut at Sandown in July. The son of Lawman is from a family of middle-distance winners but the form of his race subsequently fell apart.

Stable companion **Inverness** came with a late burst to pip Educator in a 1m maiden at Goodwood in September. He is bred to be effective over further.

the Weekend Card

Issued every Wednesday, The *Weekend Card* is our specialist publication offering professional updates, views and recommendations from our select team of experts. Available to download and through the post.

The *Card* covers the next six days racing with the emphasis firmly focused upon the key weekend action. The importance of continuity is the heartbeat of this service, so not only do you receive all the latest news on key horses from our various publications which are declared to run, but also informed comments on selected horses from previous editions.

And we also provide you with honest and accurate feedback on all the previous week's selections – win or lose.

The *Card*, which includes a quick reference sheet, is available as a download, hard copy (by post) or both and you receive a Welcome Pack when you subscribe.

One of the most popular sections in the Card is Marten's Sleeper Section.

This is currently showing a profit to level stakes of 109 points and a return on investment of 57%, while Marten's Look Ahead feature is also showing a profit to level stakes of 68 points thanks to winners that include Sonny Liston 18/1, Atrium 16/1, Reversion 16/1, Gifted Gold 12/1, Lindwall 8/1, Designer 11/2 and long-odds gamble Pride Of Hawridge 9/2 (from 16/1).

Order online at www.martenjulian.com or call the office on 01539 741 007

Martyn Meade's **Zechariah** needs to settle better if he is to get home over the Derby trip.

Aidan O'Brien appears to have the French Classics in mind for Leopardstown maiden winner **Star Of India**. Despite being by Galileo his distaff side is mainly comprised of milers.

We also need to keep an eye on Punchestown 1m maiden winner **River Thames**, a son of Churchill but from a speedy bottom line. He may struggle over more than a mile.

The trainer has a handful of unraced colts that carry a Derby entry. They include **Waterville**, a half-brother to 10 winners including Irish Oaks winner Sea Of Class and Italian Group 1 winners. He has a solid middle-distance pedigree.

So, too, does **Martinstown**, a son of Galileo and full brother to Group 2 1m 6f winner Free Wind. **Newfoundland** is an unraced full brother by Deep Impact to the ill-fated Snowfall. **Middlemarch**, by Caravaggio from the family of Bigstone, is another to watch for.

Stable companions **Anchorage** and **Bluegrass** need to progress from last season's solid efforts.

Cash should do well for David Simcock. The son of Shamardal, who surprised connections when winning on his debut at Newmarket in October, is out of a well-related winner over 1m 6f. His form held up quite well.

Jane Chapple-Hyam has ambitious plans for runaway Newmarket novice winner **Claymore** but he needs to settle if he is to stay middle distances.

Franz Strauss won what could turn out to be a decent novice contest at Newcastle in December. John and Thady Gosden's son of Golden Horn is bred to stay well and the trainer likes to introduce a few of his top-class prospects on this surface.

Stable companion **Knight Of Honour**, third on his debut at Leicester in October, would not carry a Derby entry unless greater things were expected of him but of more interest may be **Magisterial**, who stepped up from a Newmarket fourth in September to gallop clear and win a 1m novice stakes at Haydock in October.

Oisin Murphy was very complimentary about the horse afterwards and this full brother to middle-distance winner Flaunt can improve for a distance of ground. He is one to note as a possible successor to Stradivarius for owner Bjorn Nielsen.

The Gosdens will also be looking forward to seeing 1m Yarmouth maiden winner **Mighty Ulysses** back in action. The son of Ulysses is from the family of Rebecca Sharp and he overcame a slow start and then a reluctance to settle to quicken through to win by three and a quarter lengths.

The form didn't add up to much but this colt was very green and he unleashed an eye-catching turn of foot. It will be interesting to see where he is placed.

Frantastic, a full brother to Cracksman, overcame inexperience to win a 1m novice at Newcastle with plenty in hand.

Joseph O'Brien's **Herring Island** was all out to beat the 85-rated seven-race maiden Barud by a neck at Navan in October. This display was workmanlike at best, but as a half-brother to a bumper and hurdle winner he can improve for a step up in trip.

The trainer should also win races with **Como Park**, by Camelot out of a Dansili mare, **Nusret**, a son of Golden Horn and half-brother to seven winners out of a Daylami mare, the Zoffany colt **Point King** and **Vega Magnifico**, a once-raced son of Lope De Vega.

Brother Donnacha O'Brien has made a Derby entry for **First Emperor**, a three-parts brother to the top-class Snow Lantern. He is evidently deemed to be useful.

Subastar, winner of his sole start, a 1m maiden at Newmarket in September, trained by Roger Varian, is from the family of Dubawi and other high-class performers. He beat Dawn Of Liberation at Newmarket and that form now reads well.

Subastar could be the right type for the King Edward VII Stakes.

The trainer will also win more races with **Eldar Eldarov**, who overcame greenness to win an extended 1m maiden at Nottingham in October. The son of Dubawi comes from one of Kirsten Rausing's most successful families and should relish a step up in trip.

Stable companion **Eydon** shaped well when making the frame in his two starts at Newcastle.

The Queen's **Educator**, trained by William Haggas, can improve for a step up to middle distances as should **Lysander**, who shaped well when third on his Newbury debut in October. I suspect better was expected from **Soulcombe** when he ran down the field on his debut at Newmarket in October.

David Menuisier is nobody's fool and he is sure to win races with **Sir Bob Parker**, who ran second on his sole start at Saint-Cloud last November. The son of Siyouni is from a family deep with stamina and he is one to keep in mind for staying races later in the year.

The same trainer will win races with **Lionel**. The son of Lope De Vega showed plenty of ability when coming from a poor position to finish second in a 1m novice in heavy ground at Newbury. His dam Gretchen won the Group 2 Park Hill Stakes and is a half-sister to Irish St Leger winner Duncan, 2m 2f Doncaster Cup winner Samuel and other useful performers.

This colt is bred to thrive over a distance of ground. I expect him to prove very useful.

West Wind Blows overcame a troubled run to win an extended 1m 2f novice stakes at Newcastle for Simon and Ed Crisford in December. He is by Teofilo out of a Prix de Diane winner.

Finally Ismail Mohammed has made a Derby entry for the unraced **Sea Stone**, a son of Sea The Stars out of Fillies' Mile winner White Moonstone.

Conclusion

Point Lonsdale and Luxembourg will probably be aimed at Epsom if things go well for them at Newmarket. Both colts should stay the trip.

There is sufficient stamina in the pedigree of Coroebus to raise hopes he will stay but the one that looks destined to appear, for all manner of reasons, is Reach For The Moon. He has a strong middle-distance pedigree but he has been beaten in a Group 2 and needs to improve. There are, though, rational grounds for expecting that to happen when he is stepped up in trip.

There are any number of lightly raced and unraced types that could emerge through the ranks. Among them we should keep an eye on New London, Walk Of Stars, Desert Crown, Waterville, Newfoundland, Bluegrass, Middlemarch and Magisterial.

It's difficult, but I suggest Reach For The Moon and Coroebus, at 10/1 and 20/1 respectively.

THE 1000 GUINEAS PREVIEW

I struggle to warm to the 1000 Guineas as a betting medium, ever since Homecoming Queen made all to win the race by nine lengths in 2012.

In fact I have never left a racecourse in such a bad frame of mind as I did that day. Here was a filly who had raced no fewer than 13 times, only breaking her duck on her eighth start in a 7f nursery at Fairyhouse in the September of her two-year-old campaign.

Two outings later she won a Listed race and in her race before the Guineas she won a Group 3 at Leopardstown by a neck, rated at the time on 105.

There were extenuating circumstances that day – there was a lengthy delay when a filly was fatally injured in the stalls – but my bad mood was then exacerbated upon hearing from a well-informed layer on the rails that the chauffeur of one of the owners had backed her to win a sizeable sum at around 40/1.

The result, especially given the substantial margin of victory, made an utter mockery of the hours devoted to my preview. I should add that I am the first to respect that a horse is made up of flesh and blood and we are not dealing with automatons, but even allowing for all that this was a bitter pill to swallow.

The filly was well beaten in her next two starts and to this day I struggle to come to terms with that extraordinary performance.

Others have also been quite hard to find, even though they have come from top yards.

Billesdon Brook may have surprised a few people when winning at 66/1 in 2018, although in her case I gave the filly a very good chance based on the manner in which she had won a nursery at Goodwood the previous August.

I acknowledge that she won there off 87, a long way adrift of Group 1 class, but only a filly with a special talent could have done what she did that day at Goodwood, and that if she were to replicate it she was in with a chance.

This year's 1000 Guineas market is headed by a filly who is unbeaten with rock-solid form and from a top yard.

Inspiral, a daughter of Frankel trained by John Gosden, made her debut in a 7f maiden on the July Course at Newmarket in late June. Steadily away, she was shuffled along in arrears and made progress from halfway and looked held by Calm Skies until picking up late to win by a length and a half – a victory that had not looked likely two furlongs from home.

Just less than a month later she took a step up in grade to contest the Listed Star Stakes at Sandown. Starting a well-backed even-money favourite, Frankie Dettori held her up in last place and turning for home she was still about 12 lengths off the pace until switched left for a run, whereupon she built up momentum and won going away by three and a half lengths.

Afterwards her trainer said that the filly hit the front too soon, something that her jockey was aware of having had concerns that they were too far off the pace turning for home. Once again she took a few strides to pick up.

Her next start came in September, when she stepped up to a mile for the Group 2 May Hill Stakes at Doncaster. Backed down to 2/9, she raced keenly fifth of the six runners before being switched left to pull clear and beat Prosperous Voyage, a filly rated 7lbs inferior, by three and three-quarter lengths.

Frankie Dettori said afterwards that due to the slow pace the filly had to quicken, adding that this 'wasn't her style'.

A month later Inspiral met the runner-up again in the Group 1 Fillies' Mile at Newmarket. Settled and racing alone with Cachet on the nearside, she was taken over to the main group and steadily picked up the pace to win by two and a half lengths.

Afterwards the trainer remarked on how well the filly handled the Dip and that she should get a mile and a quarter in time, possibly even a mile and a half.

Inspiral is the fourth foal of Starscope, a daughter of Selkirk who ran second to the aforementioned Homecoming Queen in the 2012 1000 Guineas. She is a three-parts sister to the 7f winner Astrologer and a half-sister to two other winners over nine furlongs.

She runs as if she will stay beyond a mile but her pedigree does not entirely back that up. She can produce a turn of foot but tends more to lengthening rather than quickening. The stiff mile clearly suits her and she appears to be an uncomplicated ride with a good attitude.

We know rather less about second favourite **Tenebrism**.

Aidan O'Brien's daughter of Caravaggio ran just twice, spaced wide apart at Naas in late March and then the Group 1 Cheveley Park Stakes in late September.

There was little evidence of what was to follow on her debut. Apparently struggling at halfway, she was then switched to the nearside and powered past her rivals to win going away by three and three-quarter lengths.

The performance was certainly impressive to the eye, but the subsequent form of those behind did not hold up and that was the last we saw of her for six months.

When she appeared in the Cheveley Park she started a weak 14/1 chance, up against 100-plus rated fillies with Group form. As on her debut she was slowly into her stride, tucked in on the rails, and her chance seemed remote two furlongs from home. Yet to the surprise of everyone, including her rider Ryan Moore, she then picked up and powered home to catch Flotus a few yards from the post.

Afterwards her trainer admitted that he had not expected his filly to overcome her lengthy lay-off, although adding that you don't get horses with her speed and turn of foot very often.

Tenebrism is a half-sister to winners over seven furlongs and an extended mile. Her dam Immortal Verse won the Group 1 Coronation Stakes and beat Goldikova in the Prix Jacques Le Marois at Deauville. She is from the family of top-class miler Last Tycoon.

The filly's running style augurs well for a step up in trip, but her breeding does not entirely endorse that theory. There is a lot of speed on both sides of her pedigree and, unlike the favourite, she has not yet raced beyond six furlongs. Yet what is greatly in her favour is that she appears to be blessed with an exceptional turn of foot.

On ratings the two fillies are assessed equal – both on 155 – and there are no collateral lines of form between them. However if she starts to find her stride approaching the Dip then I would expect her finishing kick to be too strong for the favourite – if she stays the mile.

Aidan O'Brien has a handful of less-exposed types that could become contenders.

Tuesday, a Galileo full sister to the seven-time Group 1 winner Minding and Irish 1000 Guineas winner Empress Josephine, confirmed the promise she had shown when a short-head runner-up to Discoveries in a 14-runner field at the Curragh last June when landing a 1m maiden at Naas this March.

The form is nothing special – the third was rated on 84 – but she was finding plenty in the closing stages and she could not be better bred.

The aforementioned **Discoveries**, a daughter of Mastercraftsman trained by Jessica Harrington, went on to run third to Agartha in the 7f Group 2 Debutante Stakes at the Curragh in August, but the following month reversed the form with the winner on better ground back there in the Group 1 Moyglare Stud Stakes.

The trainer attributed the reversal in form to the improved going and this full sister to the four-time Group 1 winner Alpha Centauri showed plenty of tenacity in the Moyglare. She will appreciate the step up to a mile but it may be a little later, on the summer ground, that we see the best of her.

Malavath, a daughter of Mehmas trained in France by Francis-Henri Graffard, won a 6f Group 2 in very soft ground at Chantilly in October before finishing a fast-closing second to Pizza Bianca in the Breeders' Cup Juvenile Fillies Turf after a slow start from the gate.

The Group 1 Fillies' Mile third **Cachet** – beaten a length by the winner – adds ballast to the form.

Her compatriot **Zellie**, a daughter of Wootton Bassett trained by Andre Fabre, won four of her six starts culminating in a defeat of Times Square, with the aforementioned Agartha five lengths back in fourth, in the Group 1 Prix Marcel Boussac in the mud at Longchamp.

She came from behind there to win in the style of a staying filly, but her trainer said afterwards that she would stick at a mile, or perhaps a mile and a quarter but no further.

Given how well she handled the easy ground she may stay in France, but we would have to afford her serious respect if she were to run at Newmarket.

Rosacea, trained in France by Stephane Wattel, evidently has a few issues with the stalls but that didn't stop her winning three of her four starts, showing a turn of foot to win the Group 3 Prix des Reservoirs in the mud at Deauville. She should remain competitive at a high level.

Mise En Scene, a daughter of Siyouni trained by James Ferguson, finished four and a quarter lengths behind Pizza Bianca at Del Mar. Before that she was beaten three lengths by Inspiral at Newmarket, having won her first two races at Haydock and a Group 3 at Goodwood.

This half-sister to a 1m 3f AW winner is out of an unraced half-sister to 1000 Guineas winner Speciosa from a family of middle-distance performers.

She has a few pounds to find but is bred to do so when stepped up in trip.

Sandrine looked the pick of the two-year-old fillies last summer.

Andrew Balding's daughter of Bobby's Kitten won the Albany Stakes and the Group 2 Duchess Of Cambridge Stakes at Newmarket in July before running a one-length second in the Lowther Stakes and then a very creditable third to Tenebrism in the Cheveley Park.

Sandrine achieved a useful level of form last season but like Mise En Scene she has a few pounds to find with the market leaders.

David Loughnane will place **Hello You** to win more races.

The daughter of Invincible Spirit ran second to Sandrine at Royal Ascot, when trained by Ralph Beckett, and then maintained that level of form in her four subsequent starts, finishing one and three-quarter lengths behind Mise En Scene at Goodwood, winning the Rockfel Stakes at Newmarket and ending with a good length and three-quarters fifth to Pizza Bianca at Del Mar. Her best form was shown on quick ground.

Jumbly was fourth to Hello You and Cachet in the Group 2 Rockfel Stakes at Newmarket and next time handled the soft ground well when winning the race formerly known as the Radley Stakes at Newbury very easily by four and three-quarter lengths.

It remains to be seen whether soft underfoot conditions are required for her to replicate this level of performance, but to the eye the turn of foot she showed to go clear was as impressive as anything we saw from a two-year-old filly last autumn.

Furthermore, she is bred to get further. The daughter of Gleneagles is a three-parts sister to Barn Owl, who won at 1m 3f, and a half-sister to 1m 4f winner Thorn. Her dam Thistle Bird won eight races including the Group 1 Pretty Polly Stakes at the Curragh over 1m 2f.

Jumbly is definitely Group class, with the potential and pedigree to make significant progress when stepped up to a mile and ten furlongs. She would not be out of place in the Guineas field, especially if it rode on the easy side.

Juncture, second to Agartha at Leopardstown last July, returned this spring with a six-length win in a 1m Listed race at Dundalk. Trained by Ger Lyons, a Guineas trial will set the way forward.

Stable companion **Sacred Bridge** may be the better of the two. The daughter of Bated Breath won her first four starts before finishing down the field when 13/8 favourite for the Cheveley Park Stakes.

Her jockey reported afterwards that the filly 'ran flat', but there is enough miling blood in her pedigree to raise hopes that she will stay the Guineas trip. She ran fourth in a Group 3 trial at Leopardstown in April.

Prosperous Voyage twice chased home Inspiral last autumn. She is a half-sister to three winners over a mile and a half, so watch for improvement when she steps up in trip.

Godolphin's **Wild Beauty**, who beat subsequent Breeders' Cup winner Pizza Bianca in the Grade 1 Natalma Stakes at Woodbine in September, subsequently finished three and a half lengths behind Inspiral at Newmarket. She ran seven times last season attaining a useful level of form.

The same owner's **Wild Place**, a winner over 6f at Meydan in February, is bred to improve for the step up to a mile.

Roger Varian's **Zanbaq** did well to win a messy race on her sole start last November at Kempton. The daughter of Oasis Dream is out of a sister to Group winners from the family of Group 1 Moyglare Stud Stakes and Coronation Stakes winner Rizeena.

The runner-up at Kempton is rated on 78, but Zanbaq displayed a good attitude to overcome a slow start and trouble in running and I expect her to earn black type at some stage.

Newmarket Group 3 winner **Fast Attack** isn't sure to stay the mile but Simon and Ed Crisford would not have given her an entry unless they thought something about her.

Richard Hannon has a good record in this race and dual winner **Heredia** is bred to improve for a mile. The daughter of Dark Angel is the first foal of a 1m-winning half-sister to a US 2m winner.

Take note of **Puffing**. Ralph Beckett's daughter of Kingman showed a bright turn of foot from the front of the pace to win a 7f maiden at Kempton in December. The runner-up is now an eight-race maiden, rated on 66, but the winner impressed and has a 2m winner in her family.

Sense Of Duty, a daughter of Showcasing trained by William Haggas, had subsequent winners behind her when winning a 6f maiden at Newbury in August. She looked green there, carrying her head a little high and pounding the ground, but she will stay a mile and is clearly well regarded.

Finally, **Homeless Songs** may be a late contender following her workmanlike defeat of Agartha in the Group 3 1,000 Guineas Trial at Leopardstown.

The daughter of Frankel showed a turn of foot to win there and as a half-sister to 1m 2f Listed winner Reve De Vol out of a half-sister to Group 3 winner Carla Bianca, from a middle-distance family, she should stay beyond a mile.

Conclusion

Inspiral and Tenebrism set a high standard of form.

Both fillies are unbeaten, with the former a proven Group 1 winner over the course and distance and the latter less exposed but with the potential to improve for the step up in trip. Of the two Tenebrism made the greater visual impact, coming from way off the pace to win the Cheveley Park, but Inspiral progressed with every race last season and has a tenacious style of racing.

There may be a significant challenge from France – we need to keep an eye out for Malavath and Zellie – while if the ground rides soft I will be advocating the chance of Jumbly. I think she could be quite special in the right conditions.

Of the rank outsiders I expect Puffing to prove useful, with Zanbaq and Sense Of Duty also holding Group-class potential.

I marginally favour Tenebrism over Inspiral, with Jumbly a filly to keep on your side when she encounters easy ground.

INDEX